The
Mischief
of Sin

by

Thomas Watson
Minister of the Gospel
St. Stephen's, Walbrook

Edited by Rev. Don Kistler

Soli Deo Gloria Publications
. . . for instruction in righteousness . . .

Soli Deo Gloria Publications
P.O. Box 451, Morgan, PA 15064
(412) 221-1901/ FAX 221-1902

*

The Mischief of Sin was first published in London by
Thomas Parkhurst in 1671. This Soli Deo Gloria
edition, in which grammatical, spelling, and
formatting changes have been made, is
© 1994 by Soli Deo Gloria.

*

ISBN 1-877611-85-9

*

Second Printing 1995
Third Printing 1997
Fourth Printing 1998

Contents

It Brings a Person Low.
"And were brought low for their iniquity."
Psalm 106:43

They Sin Still.
"For all this, they sinned still."
Psalm 78:32

The Last and Great Change.
"I will wait till my change come."
Job 14:14

*A Clear Description of Such Persons as shall
Have a Greater Share in Hell Torments.*
"These shall receive greater damnation."
Mark 12:40

The Mystery of the Lord's Supper.
Matthew 26:26-28

Foreword

Rev. Don Kistler, publisher of the Soli Deo Gloria line, sent me a manuscript of this wonderful work when he learned I had recently completed my own book on sin (*The Vanishing Conscience*). I had been contemplating for weeks the biblical doctrines of human depravity and divine holiness. My mind and heart were full of thoughts about the wretchedness of the human heart and the richness of God's grace.

I was therefore naturally eager to read this book— but unprepared for the sumptuous soul-feast it offered. Reading it reminded me once again how seriously the Puritans dealt with Scripture, how clearly they thought, how straightforwardly they preached, how sensibly they presented their doctrine, and how wonderfully they could convey heavenly truth through the medium of earthly language. The book enriched and expanded my own understanding of sin and grace beyond anything I could have anticipated.

Thomas Watson was without equal as a Puritan writer. His works are all practical studies of Christian doctrine. In the words of Charles Spurgeon, "Watson was one of the most concise, racy, illustrative, and suggestive of those eminent divines who made the Puritan age the Augustan period of evangelical literature. There is a happy union of sound doctrine, heart-searching experience and practical wisdom in all his works."[1] Watson's best known work, *A Body of Divinity*, is one of the finest of all classic Puritan works. *The Mischief of Sin*, though perhaps not as well known, shows with equal clarity why Watson remains one of the best loved and most significant writers of his age.

Watson is a sort of Puritan Melchizedek. His lineage, as well as the dates of his birth and death, are not precisely known. Yet he emerged out of the Puritan era to write several powerful works that continue to influence the minds and hearts of readers.

This book is one of the most difficult to obtain of all Watson's works—until now, that is. The church owes a great debt of gratitude to Don Kistler and Soli Deo Gloria for finding one copy in a library and making it available once again in this beautifully designed edition.

Thomas Watson's study of sin is profound, convicting, thought-provoking, and filled with rich spiritual insight. It distills the best attributes of Puritan writing. As devotional as it is doctrinal, as practical as it is biblically sound, and as delightful as it is convicting, this book cuts to the very heart of the biblical issues regarding sin. You cannot read it and remain indifferent toward sin in your own life.

In stark contrast to the prevailing modern attitude toward sin, Thomas Watson shows clearly that every sin is an indefensible transgression against God's holiness. He exposes the unutterable vileness of all our spiritual failings and refuses to offer excuses or rationalizations to soothe human pride or mollify the sinful ego. In

---

[1] Charles H. Spurgeon. "Brief Memoir of Thomas Watson" in Thomas Watson, *A Body of Divinity* (Edinburgh, Banner of Truth, 1958), vii.

fact, pride itself he denounces as a heinous sin.

This is such a departure from the contemporary tendency to treat evildoers as victims that you may be shocked by the contrast. But Watson presents his case so biblically and convincingly that it is impossible to argue against him.

Against the dark backdrop of sin and the utter hopelessness of the human condition, Watson displays the shining jewel of divine grace. He points to Jesus Christ as the only answer to human despair, and counsels sinners to confess their sin and seek God's mercy through His Son, Jesus Christ. Unfolding the most sublime aspects of biblical truth, Watson shows that where sin abounds, grace abounds even more.

You might be tempted to think that a book on sin must be heavy, somber reading. But instead you will find this book a tremendous uplift as your soul is infused with a holy hatred of sin and a new appreciation for the boundless riches of God's grace.

Few books have moved me as this one did. I thank God that after so many years on a library shelf, it will now be available to a new generation of readers.

John MacArthur
Sun Valley, CA
February 1994

The Epistle to the Reader

CHRISTIAN READER,

The excess of impiety which has broken down the banks of common civility and modesty at first led my thoughts to these ensuing subjects. The spirits of men are leavened with atheism, and their lives are stained with debauchery. I do not know what to call them but baptized heathens. Not long since, there was a complaint that the springs grew low. I am sure the floods of sin are risen, even to a deluge. There is a generation among us of whom I may say, as Oecumenius, they militate against religion. They are so prodigiously profane that they esteem the Bible a fable and would jeer all holiness out of the world. The Prince of the Air now works in the children of disobedience, Ephesians 2:2.

In our Savior's time, many men's bodies were possessed with the devil. But now their souls are possessed. One is possessed with a blasphemous devil, another with a spiteful devil, another with a drunken devil. This is one great sign of the approach of the last day: iniquity shall abound, Matthew 24:12. Men's lusts grown fierce and insatiable and, like imps, lie sucking them. But O how dire and tremendous will the effects of sin be! My text says, "They were brought low for their iniquity." Sin is such a trade that whoever follows is sure to break. What did Achan get by his wedge of gold? It was a wedge to cleave asunder his soul from God. What did Judas get by his treason? He purchased a halter. What did King Ahaz get by worshiping the gods of Damascus? They were the ruin of him and all Israel, 2 Chronicles 28:23. Sin is first comical and then tragical. I may fitly apply those words of Solomon to sin, Proverbs 7:26. "She hath cast down many wounded." O what a harvest of souls is the devil likely to have! Isaiah 5:14, "Hell hath enlarged itself." It is fain to make room for its guests. 'Tis matter of grief to think that the dragon should have so many followers and the Lamb so few.

Cyprian brings in the devil insulting Christ thus: "As for my followers, I never died for them as Christ has died for His. I never promised them as great a reward as Christ has done to His; yet I have greater numbers than He, and my followers venture more for me than His do for Him."

Some sin out of ignorance, yet even the blind can find the way to hell. But most sin out of choice. They know the dish forbidden, but they lust after it, though in the day they eat thereof, they shall surely die.

My design in this small treatise is to give check to sinners and sound a religious retreat in their ears, to make them return from the hot pursuit of their impieties. If notwithstanding all admonitions they will run counter to the Word, and prostitute themselves to their sordid lusts, they are suicide, and their blood will be upon their own head. What remains but that God should say in anger, as in Zachariah 11:9, "That that dieth, let it die, and that that is to be cut off, let it be cut off."

I have, at the request of some friends, made this discourse (imparted formerly to my own family) public. I acknowledge it is not inflated with rhetorical huffing and puffing, embellished with flowers of eloquence. St. Paul's preaching was not with enticing words of wisdom but in the demonstration of the Spirit and power, 1 Corinthians 2:4. Plainness is ever best in beating down sin. When a wound festers, it is fitter to lance it than to embroider it with silk or lay vermilion upon it.

Reader, that God will bless these few meditations to you, and make them operative upon your heart, shall be the prayer of him who is your friend, studious of your eternal welfare,

Thomas Watson

1

The Mischief of Sin

It Brings a Person Low.

"And were brought low for their iniquity."
Psalm 106:43

If the Scripture is a spiritual rosary or garden, as St. Chrysostom said, the book of Psalms is a knot in this garden set with fragrant flowers. Luther called the Psalms a little Bible. The Psalms make sweeter music than ever David's harp did. They are calculated for every Christian's condition, and may serve either for illumination or consolation.

In this Psalm, David sets down the sins of the people of Israel.

First, in general. Verse 6, "We have sinned with our fathers." The examples of fathers are not always to be urged. Shall we not be wiser than our fathers? Fathers may err. Sometimes, it is better for a son to take his land from his father than his religion, 2 Chronicles 29:6.

Second, David makes a particular enumeration of their sins.

1. Their forgetfulness of God. Verse 13, "They soon

forgot His works." Or, as it is in the original, they made haste to forget his works. The Lord wrought a famous miracle for them, verse 11. He drowned Israel's enemies and Israel drowned His mercies. Our sins and God's kindnesses are apt quickly to slip out of our memory. We deal with God's mercies as with flowers. When they are fresh, we smell them and put them in our bosom. But within awhile, we throw them away and mind them no more. They made haste to forget His works.

2. Their inordinate lusting. Verse 14, "They lusted exceedingly in the wilderness." They were weary of the provision which God sent them miraculously from heaven. They grew dainty. They wept for quails. They were not content that God should supply their wants, but they would have Him satisfy their lusts too. God let them have their requests. They had quails, but in anger. "He sent leanness to their souls." In other words, He sent a plague whereby they pined and consumed away.

3. Their idolatry. Verse 19, "They made a calf in Horeb." They framed for themselves a god of gold and worshiped it. The Scripture calls idols "Bosheth," a shame, Hosea 9:10. For this, God disclaimed them from being His people. Exodus 32:2, "Thy people have corrupted themselves." Formerly God called them His people, but now He does not say to Moses "My people," but "thy people."

4. Their infidelity. Verse 24, "They believed not His Word, but murmured." They did not think that God would subdue their enemies and bring them into that pleasant land flowing with milk and honey. And this unbelief broke forth into murmuring. They wished

they had made their graves in Egypt, Exodus 16:3. When men begin to distrust the promise, then they quarrel at Providence. When faith grows low, passions grow high. For these things, God stretched out His hand against them, as it is in the text, "And they were brought low for iniquity."

The words branch themselves into two parts.

1. Israel's misery. "They were brought low." Some expositors translate it, "They waxed lean." The Hebrew and Septuagint render it, "They were humbled."

2. The procuring cause of it, "for their iniquity."

DOCTRINE. The proposition resulting from the text is that sin brings a person low. Psalm 147:6, "The wicked He casteth down to the ground." Sin is a planet of a bad aspect. Jeptha said to his daughter when she met them with timbrel and dances, Judges 11:35, "Alas my daughter, thou hast brought me very low." So a man may say to his sin, "Alas, my sin, thou hast brought me very low."

Sin is the great leveler. It brings a family low. It cuts off the arm and dissolves the pillars thereof. 1 Samuel 2:29, "Wherefore kick ye at my sacrifice?" Verse 31, "Behold, the days come that I will cut off thy arm; and the arm of thy father's house, that there shall not be an old man in thy house." Which threatening God made good when He cut off Eli's two sons and put the other sons from the priesthood.

Sin brings a kingdom low. 1 Samuel 15:19, "Wherefore didst not thou obey the voice of the Lord, but didst evil in His sight?" Verse 28, "The Lord hath rent the kingdom of Israel from thee this day."

Sin breaks the axletree of church and state. Hosea

13:1, "When Ephraim spake trembling, he exalted himself, but when he offended in Baal, he died." The tribe of Ephraim carried a majesty with it and was superior to the ten tribes. When Ephraim spoke, he struck an awe and terror into others, but when he offended in Baal, he died. When once he fell from God by idolatry, he degraded himself of his honor. His strength and glory came to nothing. Now every puny adversary insulted him, as the hare will tread upon a dead lion.

Among the many threatenings against sin, Deuteronomy 28:43, "Thou shalt come down very low." And in the text this threatening is exemplified and made good, "They were brought low for their iniquity." That I may amplify and illustrate the proposition, I shall show:

1. How many ways sin brings a man low.
2. Why sin must bring a man low.

HOW MANY WAYS SIN BRINGS A MAN LOW

1. *Sin brings a man low in God's esteem.* The sinner sets a high price upon himself, Proverbs 26:16, but God has low thoughts of him, and looks upon him with a despicable eye. Daniel 11:21, "And in his estate, shall stand up a vile person." Who was this spoken of? It was Antiochus Epiphanes. He was a king, and his name signifies "illustrious," and by some he was worshiped. Yet in God's account he was a vile person. The Psalmist speaking of the wicked says, "They are become filthy," Psalm 14:3. In the Hebrew, it is "they are become stinking." That you may see how low a sinner is fallen

in God's account, the Lord compares him to dross, Psalm 119:119; to chaff, Psalm 1:4; to a pot boiling with scum, Ezekiel 24:6; to a dog, 2 Peter 2:22, which under the Law was unclean; to a serpent, Matthew 23:33, which is a cursed creature. Nay, he is worse than a serpent, for the poison of a serpent is what God has put into it, but a wicked man has that which the devil has put into him. Acts 5:3, "Why hath Satan filled thy heart?"

Caelius Rhodiginus reports of an ancient woman who had always used flattering glasses. By chance, she saw her face in a true glass and fell mad. A sinner is well-conceited of himself while he dresses himself by the flattering glass of presumption. But if he knew how loathsome and disfigured he was in God's eye, he would abhor himself in the dust.

2. *Sin brings a man low in his intellectual parts.* It has eclipsed the rational part. Darkness is upon the face of this deep. Since the Fall, the lamp of reason burns dim. 1 Corinthians 13:9, "We know but in part." There are many knots in nature that are not easy to untie. Why should the Nile overflow in summer when, by the course of nature, waters are lowest? Why should the loadstone rather draw iron than gold, a more noble metal? "What way the light is parted?" Job 38:24. "How do the bones grow in the womb?" Ecclesiastes 11:5. Many of these are paradoxes we do not understand. The key of knowledge is lost in the tree of knowledge.

We are enveloped with ignorance especially in sacred matters. "The sword is upon our right eye," Zachariah 11:16. What a little of the sea will a nutshell hold? How little of God will our intellect contain? Job

11:7, "Canst thou find out the Almighty unto perfection?" Who can fully unriddle the Trinity or fathom the mystery of the hypostatic union? And alas, as to salvific, heart-transforming knowledge, how are we to seek till God's Spirit lights our lamp! 1 Corinthians 2:14.

3. *Sin brings a man low in affliction.* That is the meaning of Psalm 107:39, "They were brought low for their iniquity." Adam's sin brought him low; it banished him out of paradise. 2 Chronicles 28:18, "In those days, God cut Israel short." Sin makes God cut a people short in their spiritual and civil liberties. Sin is the womb of sorrow and the grave of comfort. Sin turns the body into a hospital. It causes fevers, ulcers, and apoplexy.

Sin buries the name, melts the estate, pulls away near relations like limbs from our body. Sin is the trojan horse out of which a whole troop of afflictions comes. Sin drowned the old world and burnt Sodom. Sin made Zion sit in Babylon. Lamentations 1:8, "Jerusalem hath grievously sinned, therefore she is removed." Sin shut up God's bowels. Lamentations 2:21, "Thou hast killed and not pitied." Israel sinned and did not repent, and God killed and did not pity. Sin is the great humbler. Did not David's sin bring him low? Psalm 38:3, "There is no rest in my bones because of my sin." Did not Manasseh's sin bring him low? It changed his royal crown into fetters, 2 Chronicles 33:11. For sin, God turned King Nebuchadnezzar to grass, Daniel 4:33.

Sin is like the Egyptian reed—too feeble to support us but sharp enough to wound us. Jeremiah 2:16, "The children of Noph and Tahapanes have broke the crown of thy head." The Egyptians were not a warlike but a womanish people, imbecilic and weak, yet these were too hard for Israel and made a spoil of her. Verse 17: "Hast thou not procured this to thyself?" Is it not your sin that has brought you low?

Nay, sin not only brings us low but it embitters affliction. Sin puts teeth into the cross. Guilt makes affliction heavy. A little water is heavy in a lead vessel, and a little affliction is heavy in a guilty conscience.

4. *Sin brings one low in melancholy.* This is a black humor seated chiefly in the brain. Some have strange and dismal concepts, fancying their bodies to be made all of glass, and that if any one touches them, they shall break. Melancholy clothes the mind in sable. It puts a Christian out of tune so that he is not fit for prayer or praise. Lute strings will not sound when wet, nor can one under the power of melancholy make melody in his heart to the Lord, Ephesians 5:19. When the mind is troubled, it is unfit to go about work.

Melancholy disturbs reason and weakens faith. Satan works much on this tempter. It is the bath of the devil. He bathes himself with delight in such a person. Through the black spectacles of melancholy, everything appears black. When a Christian looks upon sin, he says, "This Leviathan will devour me." When he looks upon ordinances, these will serve to increase his guilt. When he looks upon affliction, this gulf will swallow him. Melancholy creates fears in the mind. It excites jealousies and misprisions. I may allude to Psalm 53:5, "There were they in great fear where no fear was."

5. *Sin brings a man low in spiritual plagues.* It brings
many a one to a seared conscience, to final induration.
Isaiah 29:10: "The Lord hath poured out upon you the
spirit of a deep sleep, and hath closed your eyes." Men
are brought low indeed when the sound of Aaron's
bell will not awaken them. No sermon will stir them.
They are like the blacksmith's dog that can lie and
sleep near the anvil when all the sparks fly about.
Conscience is in a lethargy. Once a man's speech is
gone and his feeling lost, he draws on apace to death.
So when the checks of conscience cease and a man is
sensible neither of sin nor wrath, you may ring out the
bell. He is past hope of recovery. Thus some are
brought low, even to a reprobate sense. This is the
threshhold of damnation.

6. *Sin brings a man low in temptation.* Paul began to
be proud, and he had a messenger of Satan to buffet
him, 2 Corinthians 12:7. Some think it was a visible ap-
parition of Satan tempting him to sin. Others, that the
devil was now assaulting Paul's faith, making him believe he was a hypocrite. Satan laid the train of temptation to blow up the fort of his grace. And this temptation was so sore that he called it "a thorn in the flesh."
It put him to much anguish. Such temptations the
godly often fall into. They are tempted to question the
truth of the promises or the truth of their own graces.
Sometimes they are tempted to blasphemy, sometimes
to self-murder. Thus, they are brought low; they are
almost gone and ready to give consent. The devil nib-
bles at their heel, but God wards off the blow from
their head.

7. *Sin brings one low in desertion.* This is an abyss indeed. Psalm 88:6, "Thou hast laid me in the lowest pit." Desertion is a short hell. Song of Solomon 5:6, "My beloved hath withdrawn himself and was gone." Christ knocked, but the spouse was loath to rise off her bed of sloth and open to Him immediately. When the devil finds a person sleeping he enters. But when Christ finds him sleeping, He is gone. And if this Sun of righteousness withdraws His golden beams from the soul, darkness follows. Desertion is the arrow of God shot into the soul.

Job 6:4, "The arrows of the Almighty are within me, the poison whereof drinketh up my spirit." The Scythians, in their wars, used to dip their arrows in the blood and gall of asps that the venemous heat of them might torture the enemy all the more. So the Lord shot His poisoned arrows of desertion at Job, under the wounds whereof his spirit lay bleeding. God is called a light and a fire in Scripture. The deserted soul feels the fire but does not see the light. So dreadful is this that the most tormenting pains—stone, collick, or urinary infections—are but a pleasure to it. All the delights under the sun will administer no comfort in this condition. Wordly things can no more relieve a troubled mind than a silk stocking can ease a broken leg. Psalm 88:15, "While I suffer thy terrors, I am distracted." Luther, in desertion, was like one giving up the ghost. "He had no blood seen in his face, nor was heard to speak, but his body seemed dead," as one wrote in a letter to Melancthon.

8. *Sin brings many low in despair.* This is a gulf that none but reprobates fall into. Jeremiah 18:11, "Thou

saidst, there is no hope." Despair is a devouring of salvation. It is a millstone tied about the soul that sinks it in perdition. Despair looks on God not as a Father but as a Judge. It refuses the remedy. Other sins need Christ; despair rejects Him. It closes the orifice of Christ's wounds that no blood will come out to heal. This is the voice of despair, "My sin is greater than the mercy of God can pardon." It makes the wound broader than the plaster.

Despair is a God-affronting sin. It is sacrilege; it robs God of His crown-jewels, His power, goodness, and truth. How Satan triumphs to see the honor of God's attributes laid in the dust by despair! Despair casts away the anchor of hope, and then the soul must sink. What will a ship do in a storm without an anchor? Despair locks men up in impenitency. I have read of one Hubertus who died despairing. He made his will after this manner, "I yield my goods to the King, my body to the grave, my soul to the devil." Isaiah 38:18, "They that go down into the pit cannot hope for Thy truth." They who go down into this pit of despair cannot hope for the truth of God's promise. And this despair grows at last into horror and raving.

9. *Sin brings a man without repentance into the bottomless pit, and then he is brought low indeed.* Sin draws hell at the heels of it. Psalm 9:7, "The wicked shall be turned into hell." Not to speak of the punishment of loss, which divines think is the worst part of hell: the being separated from the beatific sight of God, "in whose presence is fullness of joy," Psalm 16:11. The punishment of sense is bad enough. The wrath will come upon sinners to the uttermost, 1 Thessalonians 2:16.

If when God's anger is kindled but a little, and a spark of it flies into a man's conscience in this life, it is so terrible, what will it be when He stirs up all His wrath? Psalm 78:38. How sad was it with Spira when he only sipped of the cup of wrath. He was a very anatomy. His flesh consumed, he became a terror to himself. What is it then to lie steeping in hell?

Some may ask where the place of hell is? But as Chrysostom said, "Let us not be inquisitive where it is, but rather let our care be to escape it." But, to satisfy curiosity, hell is some infernal place. It lies low. Proverbs 15:24: "Hell beneath." Hesiod said, "Hell is as far under the earth as heaven is above it."

CONSIDER THE PLURALITY OF HELL TORMENTS

In bodily sickness, seldom above one disease at a time troubles the patient—the stone or gout—but in hell, there is a diversity of torments. There is:

1. Darkness, Jude 13. Hell is a dark region.

2. There are bonds and chains, 2 Peter 2:4. God has golden cords, which are His precepts tying men to duty, and iron chains, which are partly His decree in ordaining men to destruction and partly His power in bridling and chaining them up under wrath. The binding the wicked in chains notes that the damned in hell cannot move from place to place, which might perhaps a little alleviate and abate their misery; but they shall be tied to the stake never to stir. The wicked could go from one sin to another, but in hell they shall not move from one place to another.

3. The worm that never dies, Mark 9:44. This is a self-accusing mind which is so torturing, as if a worm

full of poison were gnawing at a man's heart. Such as would not hear the voice of conscience shall be made to feel the worm of conscience.

THE SEVERITY OF HELL TORMENTS

It is expressed by a lake of fire, Revelation 20:15. Fire is the most torturing element. Nebuchadnezzar's fiery furnace was but painted fire to this. It is called "fire prepared," Matthew 25:41, as if God had been sitting down to devise some exquisite torment. Dives cried out, "O I am tormented in this flame," Luke 16:24.

1. The torments of hell shall be in every part of body and soul. The body shall be tormented. That body which was so tender and delicate that it could not bear heat or cold shall suffer in every part. The eyes shall be tormented with sights of devils, the ears with the hideous shrieks of the damned. The tongue that was fired with passion shall now have fire enough. Luke 16:24: "Send Lazarus, that he may dip the tip of his finger in water and cool my tongue."

All the powers of the soul shall be tormented. The mind to apprehend divine displeasure, the memory to remember what mercies have been abused, what means of grace have been slighted, and what a heaven is forfeited. The conscience shall be tormented with self-accusations. The sinner shall arraign himself for stifling and resisting the motions of the blessed Spirit.

The wicked shall not only be forced to behold the devil, but shall be shut up in the den with this roaring lion and he shall spit fire in their faces.

The wicked shall hear the language of hell.

Revelation 16:9: "Men were scorched with heat, and blasphemed the name of God." To hear reprobates cursing God and have one's ears chained to their oaths and blasphemies, what a hell will this be?

2. The torments of hell have no period put to them. Origen fancied a fiery stream in which the souls of sinful men, yea, devils and all, were to be purged and then pass into heaven. But the Scripture asserts that whoever is not purged from sin by Christ's blood (1 John 1:7) is to lie under the torrid zone of God's wrath to all eternity. Revelation 14:11, "The smoke of their torment ascendeth up forever and ever." The word "ever" burns hotter than the fire. At death, all our worldly sorrows die, but the torments of hell are as long-lived as eternity. Revelation 9:6, "They shall seek death, and shall not find it." Always dying, but never dead. Here the wicked thought a prayer was long, a Sabbath long, Amos 8:5, but how long will it be to lie in hell forever!

3. The pains of hell are without intermission. If a man is in pain, yet while he is asleep he does not feel it. There is no sleep in hell. What would the damned give for one hour's sleep? Revelation 4:8. "They rest not day nor night." In outward pain, there is some abatement. The burning fit is sometimes off and the patient is more at ease than he was. But the damned soul never says, "I have more ease." Those infernal pains are always acute and sharp; no cooling fits in those inflammations.

4. In hell, the wicked shall see the godly advanced to a kingdom and themselves devoted to misery. Luke 13:28, "Then shall be weeping and gnashing of teeth, when ye shall see Abraham, and Isaac, and Jacob, and

all the prophets in the kingdom of God, and you yourselves thrust out." When sinners shall see those whom
they hated and scorned to be set at Christ's right hand
and crowned with glory, and themselves cast out to the
devils; nay, when the ungodly shall see those whom
they censured and persecuted sit as their judges, and
join with Christ in condemning them. How will this
aggravate the misery of those hellish caitiffs and make
them gnash their teeth for envy? 1 Corinthians 6:2:
"Know ye not that the saints shall judge the world?"

5. In hell, the wicked shall have none to sympathize
with them. It is some comfort to have friends condole
with us in our sufferings, but the damned have none to
compassionate them. Mercy will not pity them, mercy
abused turns to fury. God the Father will not pity them;
He will laugh at them. Proverbs 1:26, "I will laugh at
your calamity." Is not this sad, for a damned soul to lie
roaring in flames and have God sit and laugh at him?
Jesus Christ will not pity the wicked. They slighted His
blood, and now His blood cries against them. The angels will not pity them. It is a desirable sight to men to
see God's justice glorified. The saints in heaven will
not pity them. They were continually persecuted by
them, and "they shall rejoice when they see the
vengeance," Psalm 58:10.

Nay, such as were their nearest relations on earth
will not pity them. The father will not pity his child in
hell nor the wife her husband. The reason is because
the saints glorified have their wills made perfectly subject to God's will, and when they see His will is done
they rejoice, though it is in the damning of their near
relations.

Does not sin, then, bring men low when it brings

them to hell? Ezekiel 32:27, "They are gone down to hell, they have laid their swords under their heads, but their iniquity shall be upon their bones." Thus I have shown you how many ways sin brings one low.

WHY SIN MUST BRING A MAN LOW

1. *Because sin is a disease, and that brings low.* Take the healthiest constitution, the most sanguine complexion, yet, if sickness gets into it, it brings the body low. The beauty withers. The silver cord begins to be loosed. So it is in spiritual things. The soul which was once of an orient brightness, the mind angelified, the will crowned with liberty, the affections as so many seraphims burning in love to God, yet by sin has become diseased, Isaiah 1:6, and this disease brings it low. The soul has fallen from its pristine dignity. It has lost its noble and sublimated operations and lies exposed (without grace) to the second death.

2. *Sin must bring a man low because the sinner enters a contest with God.* He tramples upon God's law and crosses His will. If God is of one mind, the sinner will be of another. He does all he can to spite God, Jeremiah 44:16, "As for the word which Thou hast spoken to us in the name of the Lord, we will not hearken to Thee, but we will do whatsoever thing proceedeth out of our own mouth, to burn incense to the Queen of Heaven." The same Hebrew word for sin signifies rebellion. Now, can the Lord endure to be thus saucily confronted by proud dust? God will never let his own

creature rise up in arms against Him. He will pull
down the sinner's plumes and bring him low. God is
called *El Elim,* the mighty of mighties. Psalm 18:26,
"With the froward, Thou wilt show Thyself froward." In
the Hebrew it is, "Thou wilt wrestle." And if God once
wrestles with the sinner, He will throw him to the
ground. When the angel wrestled with Jacob, he
touched only the hollow of his thigh, Genesis 32:25.
But when God wrestles with a sinner, He will rent the
caul of his heart, Hosea 3:8. The Apostle said, "It is a
fearful thing to fall into the hands of the living God,"
Hebrews 10:31. 'Tis good to fall into God's hands when
He is a friend, but it is ill falling into His hands when
He is an enemy.

3. *Sin must bring a man low because the sinner labors to
do what he can to bring God low.* He has low thoughts of
God. He slights His sovereignty, questions His truth,
looks upon all God's promises as a forged deed. The
sinner, therefore, is said to despise God, Numbers
11:20.

Again, the sinner lessens God and brings Him low
in the thoughts of others. Ezekiel 8:12, "They say, The
Lord seeth us not, the Lord hath forsaken the earth."
Do but secure yourselves from man's eye, and as for
God's taking notice of sin you need not trouble yourselves. "The Lord seeth you not, He hath forsaken the
earth." Zephaniah 1:12, "They say the Lord will not do
good, neither will He do evil." If you serve Him, you
must not look for reward; and if you do not serve Him,
you need not fear punishment. Malachi 2:17, "Ye say,
Everyone that doth evil is good in the sight of the
Lord, and He delighteth in them: or where is the God

of judgment?" Here they blemish God's sanctity. God is
not so holy, but He bears as much favor to the wicked
as to the good, saying, "Where is the God of judgment?" Here they tax His justice. It is as if they had
said, "God does not order things rightly. He does not
weigh matters impartially in an equal balance."

"Where is the God of judgment?" Thus a sinner
eclipses the glory of the Godhead and labors to bring
God low in the thoughts of others.

And besides, he does what in him lies to extirpate a
Deity. He wishes there were no God. He says, "Cause
the holy One of Israel to cease," Isaiah 30:11. A wicked
man would not only unthrone God, but "unbe" God. If
he could help it, God would no longer be God. Now, if
a sinner is this impious as to endeavor to bring God
low, no wonder if God brings him low. Nahum 1:19, "I
will make thy grave, for thou art vile. I will bring thee
(O Sennacherib) from the throne to the tomb. I will
kick thee into thy grave." And Obadiah 4, "Though
thou set thy nest among the stars, thence will I bring
thee down, saith the Lord.

4. *Sin must bring a person low because sin is the only
thing God has an antipathy against.* The Lord does not
hate a man because he is poor or despised. You do not
hate your friend because he is sick. But that which
draws forth the keeness of God's hatred is sin.
Jeremiah 44:4, "Do not do this abominable thing
which I hate." Now, for anyone to espouse that which
God's soul hates, it must undo him at last. Is that subject likely to thrive whom his prince hates? The cher-
ishing and countenancing of sin makes the fury come
up in God's face, Ezekiel 38:16. And, if His wrath is

once kindled, it burns to the lowest hell. The Psalmist said, "Who can stand before His cold?" Psalm 147:17, but rather who can stand before His heat? Isaiah 33:14.

5. *Sin must bring the sinner low because it exposes him to God's curse, and God's curse blasts wherever it comes.* Deuteronomy 28:15-16, "If thou wilt not harken to the voice of the Lord, all these curses shall come upon thee. Cursed shalt thou be in the city, and cursed shalt thou be in the field, cursed shall be thy basket and thy store." The curse of God haunts the sinner wherever he goes. If he is in the city, it spoils his trade. If he is in the country, it destroys his crop.

God's curse drops poison into everything. It is a moth in the wordrobe, a plague among the cattle, rot among the sheep. If the flying roll of curses enters into a man's house, it consumes the timber and walls of it, Zechariah 5:4. When Christ cursed the figtree, it immediately withered, Matthew 21:19. Men's curses are insignificant—they shoot without bullets. But Numbers 22:6 says, "He whom Thou cursest is cursed." God's curse kills, Psalm 27:22, "They that are cursed of Him shall be cut off." If all God's curses are leveled against the sinner, then he must be brought low.

USE 1. OF INFORMATION

BRANCH 1. See then from this that God's punishing either a person or a nation is not without a cause. A father may chastise his son out of a humor when there is no cause, but God never punishes without a just cause. He does it not purely to show His sovereignty, or because He takes pleasure to bring His creatures low. Lamentations 3:33, "He doth not willingly afflict," or, as it is in the Hebrew, "from the heart." But there is some impellent cause. "They were brought low for their iniquity."

Cyprian writes this concerning the persecution of the Church under the Emperor Valerian. "We must confess that this sad calamity, which has, in a great part wasted our churches, has risen from our own intestine wickedness, while we are full of avarice, ambition, emulation, etc." Jeremiah 4:17, "As keepers of a field, are they against her round about." As horses or deer in a field are so enclosed with hedges and so narrowly watched that they cannot get out, so Jerusalem was so besieged with enemies and watched that there was no escape for her without danger of life. Verse 18, "Thy way and thy doings have procured these things unto thee, this is thy wickedness."

As we used to say to children when they were sick, "This is because of the green fruit you have eaten, or from your going out in the snow," so God says, "This is your wickedness." Jeremiah 30:15, "Why criest thou for thy affliction, because thy sins were increased, I have done these things unto thee." The sword that wounds you is of your own whetting. The cords that pinch you are of your own twisting. Thank your sin for all. 1 Corinthians 11:30, "For this cause many are sick, and weak, and many fall asleep." The Church at Corinth was punished with corporal death because of coming unworthily to the Lord's Table and profaning the body and blood of the Lord.

The abuse of holy things incenses God. Nadab and Abihu found the flames of wrath hot about the altar,

Leviticus 10:1-2. So that there is still a cause why God brings any person low. There is no reason why God should love us, but there is a great deal of reason why God should punish us. "They were brought low for their iniquity."

BRANCH 2. See from this what a mischievous thing sin is—it brings a person and a nation low. Hosea 14:1, "Thou hast fallen by thy iniquity." Sin lays men low in the grave, and in hell too, without repentance. Sin is the Achan that troubles. It is the gall in our cup and the gravel in our bread, Proverbs 20:17. Sin and punishment are linked together with Adamantine chains. Sin is the Phaeton that sets the world on fire. It is a coal that not only blackens but burns. Sin runs men into the briars. Job 30:7, "Among the bushes they brayed." Sin conjures up all the winds. All the crosses which befall us, all the storms in conscience, sin raises them. Never let anyone think to rise by sin, for the text says that it brings him low.

Sin first tempts and then damns. It is first a fox and then a lion. Sin does to a man as Jael did to Sisera. She gave him milk, but then she brought him low. Judges 5:26-27, "She put her hand to the nail, and with the hammer she smote Sisera, she smote off his head; when she had pierced and stricken through his temples, at her feet he bowed." Sin first brings us pleasures which delight and charm the senses, and then comes with its nail and hammer. Sin does to the sinner as Absalom did to Amnon. When his heart was merry with wine, then he killed him, 2 Samuel 13:28. Sin's last act is always tragic.

How evil a thing is sin that it not only brings a people low, but it makes God delight in bringing them low. Ezekiel 5:13, "I will cause my fury to rest upon them, and I will be comforted." God does not take delight in punishing. Judges 10:16, "His soul was grieved for the misery of Israel." He is like a father who chastises his child with tears. But God was so provoked with the Jews that it seemed a delight to Him to afflict. "I will cause My fury to rest upon them, and I will be comforted." Oh, what a venomous, accursed thing sin is that makes a merciful God take comfort in the destruction of His own creature!

BRANCH 3. See, then, what little cause any have to wonder that they are brought low. As the Apostle said, 1 Peter 4:12, "Think it not strange concerning the fiery trial." So do not think it strange if you are as full of eclipses and changes as the moon. Do not wonder if you are under the black rod. A sick man may as well wonder that he is in pain as a sinful man wonder that he is afflicted. Do not vapors cause thunder? Is it a wonder to hear God's thundering voice after the hellish vapors of our sins have been sent up? Sin is a debt. It is set out in Scripture by a debt of ten thousand talents, Matthew 18:24. Is it a wonder for a man who is in debt to be arrested? Never wonder that God arrests you with His judgments when you are so deeply in arrears.

Sin is a walking contrariness to God. And if men walk contrary to God, is it any wonder if God walks contrary to them? Leviticus 26:17, "If ye will walk contrary to Me, then I will also walk contrary to you, and I even I will chastise you seven times more for your sins." Oh, sinner, do not wonder that it is so bad with you, but rather wonder that it is no worse! Are you in the deep of affliction? It is a wonder you are not in the deep of hell! If Jesus Christ was brought low, is it a wonder that you are brought low?

Christ was brought low in poverty. The manger was His cradle. The cobwebs were His curtains.

He was brought low in temptation. Matthew 4:1, "He was led into the wilderness to be tempted of the devil." No sooner was Christ out of the water of baptism than He was in the fire of temptation. Only His Godhead was too strong a bulwark for Satan's fiery darts to enter.

He was brought low in His agonies. He sweat blood in the garden. He shed blood on the cross. If Christ was brought low, who knew no sin, do you wonder that you are brought low, who are so full of sin? Lamentations 3:39, "Why doth a living man complain, a man for the punishment of his sin?" What, a sinner, and you wonder or murmur that you are afflicted? Sin as naturally draws punishment to it as the magnet draws iron.

BRANCH 4. See the text fulfilled this day in our eyes. Sin has brought our nation low. We are falling down, if not collapsed. We do not lack for sin. There is a spirit of wickedness in the land. Ours are mighty sins, Amos 5:12; bloody sins, Hosea 4:2. The sins of Denmark, Spain, France, and Italy are translated into English. We have many Sodoms among us, and may fear to have the line of confusion stretched over us. By our impieties and blasphemies, we have sounded a trumpet of rebellion against heaven. Were our sins engraven upon our foreheads, we would be ashamed to look up.

Men invent new sins. Romans 1:30, "inventors of
evil things." Some invent new errors; others invent new
snares. This age exceeds former ages in sinning. As it is
with trades, there may be old trades, but there are
some new tradesmen now who have grown more dex-
terous and cunning in their trade than they were in
former times. So it is with sin. Sin is an old trade, but
there are person now alive who are more skilled in the
trade, and have grown more expert in sin, than those
who are dead and gone. In former times, sinners were
bunglers at sin compared to what they are now. They
are cunning at self-damnation. Jeremiah 4:22, "Wise to
do evil." The devil's mint is going every day, and sin is
minted faster than money. People sin with greediness,
Ephesians 4:19. They drink iniquity like water, Job
15:16. They have grown rampant in wickedness, having
laid aside the veil of modesty. Zephaniah 3:5, "The unjust knows no shame." We read that Nebuchadnezzar
had the heart of a beast given to him, Daniel 4:16. If all
who have the hearts of beasts had the faces of beasts,
men would grow very scarce.

And if sin is so high, well may it bring us low. While
the body is in a hectic fever it cannot thrive. The body
political, being in this burning fever of sin, must waste
away. Has not sin brought us low? What wars, pesti-
lences, and fires have broken out among us? The
splendor and magnificence of the city was brought low
and laid in ashes.

Sin has brought us low in our reputation. Proverbs
14:34, "Sin is a reproach to any people." Time was
when God made the sheaves of other nations do obei-
sance to our sheaf, Genesis 37:7. But our pristine fame
and renown is eclipsed. Malachi 2:2, "I have made you

base and contemptible." Trading is brought low. Many
men's estates are boiled to nothing, their gourd is
withered. Their jar of oil fails. Ruth 1:21, "I went out
full, but the Lord hath brought me home empty." Sin
has brought other nations low, and do we think to escape better than they?

Salvian observes that in Africa, when the Church of
God had degenerated from its purity, the land
abounded in vice and was sick of a pleurisy of sin.
Then the vandals entered Africa and the enemy's
sword let them bleed. Numbers 32:23, "Be sure your
sin will find you out." Like a bloodhound, it will pursue
you.

WHAT ARE THOSE SINS WHICH HAVE BROUGHT THIS CITY AND NATION SO LOW?

1. The first sin that has brought us low is pride.
Proverbs 29:23, "A man's pride shall bring him low."
Pride runs in the blood. Our first parents aspired to
Deity. They did not content themselves to know God,
but they would be as knowing as God. St. Austin calls
pride the mother of all sin. The Persian kings would
have their image worshiped by all who came into
Babylon. Sapor writes of himself as brother to the sun
and moon, and partner with the stars. Caligula the
Emperor commanded himself to be adored as a god.
He caused a temple to be erected for him. He used to
have the most costly fowls sacrificed to him. Sometimes
he would sit with a golden beard and a thunderbolt in
his hand like Jupiter, and sometimes with a trident like

Neptune.

Some persons would be more deserving if, as Solon
said, we could pluck the worm of pride out of their
head. Pride discolors our virtues and poisons our mercies. The higher we lift ourselves up in pride, the lower
God casts us down. Proverbs 15:25, "The Lord will de-
stroy the house of the proud."

There is a spiritual pride, which is three-fold:

1. Some take pride in their parts. The Lord enriches them with wit and parts suitable to the places He
calls them to, and pride fumes from their heart into
their head and makes them giddy. Herod was proud of
the oration he made, and assumed that glory to himself which he should have given to God. His pride
brought him low. "He was eaten of worms," Acts 12:23.

2. Some take pride in their duties. This worm
breeds in sweet fruit. They have said so many prayers,
heard so many sermons. Luke 18:12, "I fast twice a
week." Now they think they have made God amends.
He is beholden to them and they shall be accepted for
their religious performances. What is this but pride? Is
this not to make a Christ of our duties? The devil destroys some by making them neglect duty, and others
by making them idolize duty. Better is that infirmity
which humbles me than that duty which makes me
proud.

3. Some take pride in their graces. This seems
strange, seeing grace is given to the humble, that any
should be proud of their graces. But pride is not from
the grace in us, but the corruption—not from the
strength of holiness, but the weakness.

Christians may be said to be proud of their grace
when they lay too much stress upon their grace. In

Matthew 26:33, Peter says, "Though all men shall be offended because of Thee, yet will not I." Here was a
double pride. First, that he thought he had more grace
than the rest of the Apostles. Second, in that he laid
much weight upon his grace, making it like the Tower
of David on which hung the shield of his hope, Song of
Solomon 4:4. He leaned more on his grace than on
Christ.

Men are proud of their grace when they slight others whom they think are inferior to them in grace.
Instead of the strong bearing the infirmities of the
weak, Romans 15:1, they are ready to despise the weak.
Our Savior saw this pride breeding in his own disciples;
therefore He cautioned them against it. Matthew
18:10, "Take heed that ye despise not one of these little
ones."

There is a carnal pride. I call it carnal because it is
conversant about carnal objects.

1. Some are proud of their bodies. Pride is seen in
long and tedious dressings. People spend that time between the comb and the glass which should be spent in
prayer and holy meditation.

Pride is seen in painting their faces, overlaying
God's work with the devil's colors. Excellence coming
from the body is the more welcome beauty.

Pride is seen in spotting themselves. Pimples in the
face show that the blood is corrupt. Spots in the face
show that the heart is corrupt. Cyprian said, "They who
paint and spot their faces may justly fear that at the
resurrection their Creator will not know them."

Pride is seen in the strange antique fashions where-
with some people dress, or rather disguise themselves.

They clothe their flesh like the rainbow with divers colors. Adam was ashamed of his nakedness; these should be ashamed of their clothing. They are so plumed and gaudily attired that they tempt the devil to fall in love with them.

2. Some are proud of their estates. Riches are fuel for pride. Ezekiel 28:5, "Thy heart is lifted up because of thy riches." Men's hearts rise with their estates like the boats on the Thames rise with the tide. Now, all this pride will bring a person low. For this sin, God strikes many with frenzy, and so levels the mountain of pride. God has stained the pride of England's glory, Isaiah 23:9. He has stripped us of our jewels. Proverbs 16:8, "Pride goes before destruction." Where pride leads the van, destruction brings up the rear.

2. Another sin which has brought us low is Sabbath profanation. The Sabbath is given as a distinctive sign between the people of God and the profane, Exodus 31:17. And among the primitive saints, when the question was asked, "Have you kept the Lord's Day?" the answer was, "I am a Christian, and I dare not omit the celebration of this day." The Lord has commanded the observation of the Sabbath under a *sub poena*. He has enclosed this day for Himself. He has set a hedge around it. "Remember the Sabbath Day to keep it holy." But how is this enclosure made common? This blessed day, which is made purposely for communion with God, has become a day of activity. People frequent the fields or taverns more than the holy assemblies. Oh, that our head were waters and our eyes a fountain of tears! Oh, that we might weep, Jeremiah 9:1, to see men pollute what God Himself has consecrated. If they are to take medicine, it must be on the Lord's Day; if they are to make feasts or visits, it must be on this day. And so, in a profane sense, they call the Sabbath a delight. Sabbath breaking is sacrilege; it is robbing God of His due.

People take that time which should be dedicated wholly to the Lord and spend it in the service of the devil and his lusts. And has not this sin brought us low? God threatens, Jeremiah 17:27, "If ye will not hearken to Me, to hallow the Sabbath Day, then I will kindle a fire." I observe that the devouring fire which broke out in London began on the Sabbath Day, as if God were telling us from heaven that He was now punishing us for our profaning His Day.

3. The third sin which has brought us low is neglect of family worship. Religion in men's families is brought low. There is no reading of Scripture. They more often look at a deck of cards than a Bible. There is no praying. It is the mark of a reprobate that "he calls not upon God," Psalm 14:4. The atheist will be sure his prayer shall not be turned into sin, for he never prays at all. The Grecians asked counsel of their feigned gods by their oracles, the Persians by their Magi, the Galls by their Druids, the Romans by their Augures. Shall pagans pray and not Christians? Creatures, by the instinct of nature, cry to God. Psalm 147:9, "The young ravens which cry." Prayer has no enemies unless they are infernal spirits, and such as are near of kin to them.

Keys that are often used are bright, but if they are laid aside and never used they grow rusty. So it is with men's hearts. If they are not used to family prayer, they will be rusted over with sin.

For this, God has brought us low. Why did He pull down many houses in this city but because they were unhallowed houses. There was no prayer in them.

How can we think to have a blessing from God if we never ask for it? God would be doing more for us than He did for His own Son. Hebrews 5:7, "In the days of His flesh, He offered up prayers, with strong cries and tears."

4. Another sin which has brought us low is covenant violation. Psalm 78:10, "They kept not the covenant of God." Verse 50, "He made a way to his anger, he spared not their souls from death." The people of Carthage were noted for covenant breaking. Oh, that this sin had died with them! Does not this poisonous weed grow in our soil? Did we not make a vow in baptism to fight under Christ's banner against the world, the flesh, and the devil? Did we not solemnly covenant to be the Lord's people, to shine in sanctity, going each one before another in an exemplary reformation? Deuteronomy 5:28-29, "They have well said, in all that they have spoken, O that there were such a heart in them, that they would fear Me and keep My commandments!" We have much conforming, but where is the reforming? Is not Jesus Christ opposed in His kingly office? This is the great controversy: Who shall reign, sin or Christ? For this, God has been like a moth to us, and we may fear lest He makes good that threat, Leviticus 26:25, "I will bring a sword that shall avenge the quarrel of My covenant."

5. Another sin which has brought us low is the

abuse of the gospel. We are sick with Israel's disease. They despised manna. Numbers 21:5, "Our soul loatheth this light bread." We have been nauseated by the Bread of Life. The gospel is the visible token of God's presence. It is the sacred conduit that empties the golden oil of mercy into us. It is the glass in which we see the face of Christ. It is the celestial banquet with which God cheers and revives the souls of His people, Isaiah 25:6. But was there not a gospel glut in England? People had itching ears and did not know what to hear. And has not our curiosity brought us to scarcity? God has no better way to raise the price of the gospel than by abating the plenty. God surely brought us low when darkness overspread our horizon, and the Lord suffered so many hundred lights to be put under a bushel at one time. The Egyptian priests of old told the people that, when any eclipse happened, the gods were angry and great miseries would follow. What sad catastrophes have ensued this spiritual eclipse is not unknown.

6. Another sin which has brought us low is covetousness. When men's spirits are low and, with the serpent, they lick the dust, then God lays them in the dust. Isaiah 57:17, "For the iniquity of his covetousness, I was wroth and smote him." Covetousness is the dropsy of the soul. Men are set upon the world when God is plucking it from them. Covetousness is a key that opens the door to further wickedness. 1 Timothy 6:10, "The love of money is the root of all evil." A covetous man will stick at no sin. This made Absalom attempt to dethrone his father. This made Adhab stone Naboth.

And what is one the better for all his wealth at death? 1 Timothy 6:10, "We brought nothing into the world, and it is certain we can carry nothing out." When the rich miser dies, what scrambling is there? His friends are scrambling for his goods, the worms are scrambling for his body, and the devils are scrambling for his soul.

This sin is most uncomely in those who profess better. They pretend to live by faith, and yet are as worldly and griping as others. These are spots in the face of religion. Jeremiah 45:5, "Seekest thou great things for thyself?" For this sin, God has brought us low. He has made our fig tree to wither and allowed the caterpillars to eat our vine.

7. Another sin which has brought us low is barrenness under the means of grace. Hosea 10:1, "Israel is an empty vine." His juice runs out only into leaves. We have had much pruning and dressing. The silver drops of heaven have fallen upon us, but we have not brought forth the fruits of humility and repentance. We can discourse of religion, but this is only to bring forth leaves, not fruit. Non-proficiency has laid us low, and we may fear it will lay us waste. God may pull up the hedge and let in a foreign wild boar.

Ursin tells us that those who fled out of England in Queen Mary's days acknowledged that that calamity befell them for their great unprofitableness under the means of grace in King Edward's days. What man will sow seed in barren ground? If the Lord lays out His cost and sees no good return, the next word will be, "Cut down the tree, why does it so uselessly occupy the ground?"

8. Another sin which has brought us low is the sin of swearing. Christ said, "Swear not at all," Matthew 5:34, and a godly man is said to fear an oath, Ecclesiastes 9:2. Truly it is a matter of tears that we can hardly go out in the streets without having our ears crucified with hearing oaths and cursings. Chrysostom spent most of his sermons at Antioch against swearers. We need many Chrysostoms nowadays to preach against this sin. This may well be called "the unfruitful work of darkness," Ephesians 5:11, for it is a sin that has neither pleasure nor profit in it. How men shoot their oaths as bullets against heaven!

I knew a great swearer, said Reverend Mr. (Robert) Bolton, whose heart Satan so filled that on his death bed he swore as fast as he could, and desired the by-standers to help him with oaths and swear for him. Will the Lord reckon with men for idle words? What will He do for sinful oaths? For every oath a man swears, God puts a drop of wrath in His vial. Nay, usually, God's judgments overtake the swearer in this life. I have read of a German boy who was given to swearing, and used to invent new oaths. The Lord put a canker into his mouth which ate out his tongue.

But, you say, it is my custom to swear and I cannot leave it.

Is this a good plea? It is as if a thief should plead for a judge not to condemn him because it is his custom to rob and steal. The judge will therefore say, "You shall rather die." This sin has brought us low. Jeremiah 23:10, "For because of swearing, the land mourneth."

9. Another sin which has brought us low, and is likely to bring us yet lower, is uncleanness. The adulterer's heart is a Mount Etna, burning with lust. Adultery is the shipwreck of chastity, the murder of conscience. It was said of Rome of old that it had become a brothel. I wish it might not be verified of many parts of this land.

Adultery is a brutish sin. Jeremiah 5:8, "They neighed every one after his neighbor's wife." It is a branded sin. It not only stigmatizes men's names, Proverbs 6:33, but God makes them carry the marks of this sin in their bodies. It is a costly sin; it proves a purgatory to the purse. Proverbs 6:26, "By means of a whorish woman, a man is brought to a piece of bread." There is no coming to a harlot but as Jupiter did to Dana, in a golden shower. It is a confounding sin.

The adulterer hastens his own death. The Romans were wont to have their funerals at the Gate of Venus Temple to signify that lust ends in death. The adulterer takes a short cut to hell. Proverbs 26:27, "Till a dart strike through his liver."

Creatures void of reason will rise up in judgment against such. The turtle dove is a hieroglyphic of chastisty. The stork comes into no nest but his own, and if any stork leaves his mate and joins with another, all the rest fall on him and pluck his feathers from him. God will chiefly punish those who walk in the lust of uncleanness, 2 Peter 2:10. This sin has brought us low. The fire of lust has kindled the fire of God's anger.

10. Another sin which has brought us low is our unbrotherly animosities. Matthew 12:25, "A Kingdom divided against itself cannot stand." The Turks pray that the Christians may be kept at variance. We have, in a great measure, fulfilled the Turks' prayer.

What seeds of dissention are sown among us! How we have crumbled into parties! One is for Paul and another for Apollo, but few, I fear, are for Christ. Our divisions have given much advantage to the Popish adversary. When there is a breach made in the wall of a castle, the enemy enters there. If the Popish enemy enters, it will be at our breaches. These divisions have cut the lock of hair where our strength laid. Cut off the top of the beech tree and the whole body of the tree withers. Divisions have taken away unity and amity. Here is the top of the beech tree cut off, and this has made us to wither swiftly.

These are the sins which have brought us low, and, if the Lord does not prevent it, are likely to bring England's gray hairs to the grave with sorrow.

BRANCH 5. Hence I infer that, if sin brings a person low, then what madness is it for anyone to be in love with sin? 2 Thessalonians 2:12, "Who take pleasure in iniquity." The devil can so cook and dress sin that it pleases the sinner's palate. But hear what Job said, Job 20:12, 14: "Though wickedness be sweet in his mouth, it is the gall of asps within him." Herodotus writes of the river Hypanis that, near the fountain, the water is sweet, but a few leagues away it is exceedingly bitter. Sin will bring one low, and who would love such an enemy? The forbidden fruit is sauced with bitter herbs. Sin is a serpent by the way that bites, Genesis 49:17. When you are about to commit sin, say to your soul as Boaz said to his kinsman, Ruth 4:4, "What day thou buyest the field, thou must have Ruth with it."

So, if you will have the seed of sin, you must have

the curse with it. It will bring you low. To love sin is to love a disease. A sinner is perfectly distracted. Solomon speaks of a generation of men thusly, "Madness is in their heart while they live," Ecclesiastes 9:3. It is true of those who love sin, that sin puts a worm into conscience, a thorn into death, yet that men should love sin shows that madness is in their heart. There is no creature who willingly destroys itself but man. Sin is a silken halter, yet he loves it. Oh, remember that saying of St. Austin, "The pleasure of sin is soon gone, but the sting remains."

BRANCH 6. See what little cause we have to envy sinners. Proverbs 3:31, "Envy thou not the oppressor." Men are high in wordly grandeur. God has given them large estates, and they sin with their estates. But though they build among the stars, God will bring them down. Ezekiel 28:18, "I will bring thee to ashes." Who would envy men their greatness when their sins will bring them low? Deuteronomy 32:35, "Their foot shall slide in due time."

There is a story of a Roman who was, by a court martial, condemned to die for breaking his rank to steal a bunch of grapes. As he was going to execution, some of the soldiers were envious that he had grapes while they had none. He said, "Do you envy me my grapes? I must pay dearly for them." So the wicked must pay dearly for what they have.

The prosperity of the wicked is a great temptation to the godly. David stumbled at it and would likely have fallen. Psalm 73:2, "My steps had well nigh slipped, for I was envious at the foolish." We are ready to murmur when we see ourselves low, and envy when we see the wicked high.

Sinners live in a serene climate, under a perpetual calm. Psalm 73:5, "They are not in trouble as other men, their eyes stand out with fatness." It is said of Polycrates, King of Egypt, that he never met with any cross in his life. And Alexander, hearing that Parmenio, his general, had won the victory, and that his young son Alexander was born the same day, prayed the gods to spice his joy with some bitterness lest he should be guilty of too much joy! But this prosperous state of the wicked is matter for pity rather than envy. Their sins will bring them low. Isaiah 14:12, "How art thou fallen from heaven, O Lucifer, Son of the Morning." 'Tis spoken of the Chaldean monarch who, though high, had a sudden change befall him. Isaiah 47:1, "Come down and sit in the dust." Babylon was the lady of kingdoms, but God says, "Sit in the dust." Go into Pistrinum, into the millhouse, verse 2, "Take the millstones and grind." So will God say to the wicked, "Come down from all your pomp and glory, sit in the dust; nay, sit among the damned and there grind at the mill." The Lord will proportion torment to all the pleasure the wicked have had. Revelation 18:7, "How much she hath lived deliciously, so much torment and sorrow give her."

BRANCH 7. See the great difference between sin and grace. Sin brings a man low, but grace lifts him high. Sin tumbles him in the ditch, but grace sets him upon the throne. Psalm 91:14, "I will set him on high, because he hath known My name."

GRACE RAISES A PERSON FOUR WAYS.

1. Grace raises his projects; his designs are high. He does not look at things which are seen, 2 Corinthians 4:18. His eye is above the stars. He aims at enjoying God. When a clumsy country bumpkin goes to the court, he is greatly taken with the gay pictures and hangings, but when a member of the king's private council passes by those things, he looks at them as scarcely worthy of his notice. His business is with the king. So a carnal mind is greatly taken with the things of the world, but a saint passes by these gay things with a holy contempt. His business is with God. 1 John 1:3, "Our communion is with the Father and His Son Jesus." A Christian of the right breed aspires after the things within the veil; his ambition is the favor of God. He looks no lower than a crown; he is in the altitudes and trades among the angels.

2. Grace raises a man's reputation. It embalms his name. 1 Samuel 18:30, "David's name was much set by," or, as the original carries it, "It was precious." Hebrews 11:2, "By faith the elders obtained a good report." How renowned were the godly patriarchs for their sanctity! Moses for his self-denial, Job for his patience, Phineas for his zeal! What a fresh perfume their names send forth to this day. A good name is a saint's heir. It lives when he is dead.

3. Grace raises a man's worth. Proverbs 12:26, "The righteous is more excellent than his neighbor." As the flower of the roses in spring, as the fat of the peace offering, as the precious stones upon Aaron's breastplate, so is a saint in God's eye. Besides the shining luster of the gold, it has an eternal worth and is of great

price and eternal value. So grace not only makes a man's name shine, it puts a real worth into him. "He is more excellent than his neighbor." A heart full of love to God is precious. It is God's delight, Isaiah 62:4; it is the apple of His eye; it is His jewel; it is His garden of spices; it is His lesser heaven where He dwells. Isaiah 57:17, "I dwell with him that is of an humble spirit."

4. Grace raises a man's privilege. It advances him into the heavenly kindred. By it he is born of God, 1 John 3:1. He is a prince in all lands, Psalm 45:16 (though in this world he is like a prince in disguise). He is higher than the kings of the earth, Psalm 89:27. He is allied to angels. In short, grace lifts a man up where Christ is, far above all heavens.

And grace raises a nation as well as a person. Proverbs 14:34, "Righteousness exalteth a nation."

BRANCH 8. If sin brings a man low, see what an imprudent choice they make who commit sin to avoid trouble. Job 36:21, "Take heed, regard not inquity; for this hast thou chosen rather than affliction." This was a false charge against Job, but many may be indicted of much folly. They choose iniquity rather than affliction. To avoid poverty, they will lie and deceive. To avoid prison, they will give in against their consciences. What imprudence is this, when sin draws such dark shadows after it and entails misery upon all its heirs and successors. By committing sin to avoid trouble, we meet with greater trouble. Origen, to save himself from suffering, sprinkled incense before the idol. Later, preparing to preach, he opened his Bible and accidentally fell upon that text in Psalm 50:16, "But to the wicked God saith, what hast thou to do to declare My statutes, or that thou shouldst take My covenant in thy mouth?" At the sight of this Scripture, he fell into a passion of weeping, and was so stricken with grief and consternation that he was not able to speak a word to the people but came down from the pulpit. Spria sinned against his conscience to save his life and estate; he chose iniquity rather than affliction, but what a hell he felt in his conscience. He professed that he envied Cain and Judas, thinking their condition to be more desirable. His sin brought him low.

Oh, what unparalleled folly is it to choose sin rather than affliction. Affliction is like a rent in a coat; sin is like a rent in the flesh. He who, to save himself from trouble, commits sin is like one who, to save his coat, lets his flesh be torn. Affliction has a promise made to it, 2 Samuel 22:28, but there is no promise made to sin, Proverbs 10:29.

Surely, then, those do ill who consult for themselves, who choose sin rather than suffering; who, to avoid a lesser evil, choose a greater; who, to avoid the stinging of a gnat, run into the paw of a lion.

BRANCH 9. If God brings His own people low for sin (Israel was brought low), then how low will He bring the wicked? David was in the deep waters and Jonah went down to the bottom of the mountains. Jeremiah was in the deep dungeon. Then what a gulf of misery shall swallow up the reprobate part of the world? God's people do not allow themselves in sin, Romans 7:15. They tremble at it. They hate it, yet they suffer. If they who blush at their failings are brought low, what will become of those who boast of their scandals? "If this be done to the green tree, what shall be done to the dry?" If the godly lie among the pots, Psalm 68:13, the wicked shall lie among the devils. "If judgment begin at the house of God, what shall be the end of them that obey not the gospel?" 1 Peter 4:17. If God mingles His people's cup with wormwood, He will mingle the sinner's cup with fire and brimstone, Psalm 11:6. If God threshes the wheat, He will burn the chaff. If the Lord afflicts those He loves, how severe will He be against those He hates? They shall feel the second death, Revelation 21:8.

USE 2. OF EXHORTATION

BRANCH 1. If sin brings a person low, then let us fear to come near sin. It will either bring us into affliction or worse. Its foul face may offend, but its breath kills. Sin is the Apollyon, the man-devourer. Oh, that we were as wise for our souls as we are for our bodies! How afraid are we of that meat which we know will bring the gout or stone, or will make our fever return. Sin is feverish meat which will put conscience into a shaking fit, and shall we not be afraid to touch this forbidden fruit? Genesis 39:9, "How can I do this great wickedness and sin against God?" When the Empress Eudoxia threatened to banish Chrysostom, he said, "Tell her I fear nothing but sin!" It was a saying of Anselm, "If hell were on one side and sin were on the other, I would rather leap into hell than willingly commit sin." Love will be apt to grow wanton if it is not poised with holy fear. No better curb or antidote against sin than fear. Deuteronomy 17:13, "They shall

fear and do no more presumptuously." If we could see
hell fire in every sin, it would make us fear to commit
it. The fiercest creatures dread fire. When Moses' rod
was turned into a serpent, he was afraid and fled from
it. Sin will prove to be a stinging serpent. Oh, fly from
it! Most people are like the leviathin, made without
fear, Job 41:33. They play upon the hole of the asp.
Sinners never fear till they feel. Nothing will convince
them but fire and brimstone.

BRANCH 2. If sin brings a person low, then when
we are brought low under God's afflicting hand, let us
behave ourselves wisely and as become Christians. I
shall show:

What we must not do when we are brought low.
When our condition is low, let not our passions be
high. Impatience is not the way to get out of trouble,
but rather to go lower into trouble. What does the
child get by struggling but more blows? Oh, do not lisp
out a murmuring word against God! Murmuring is the
scum which boils off from a discontented heart. Psalm
39:9, "I was dumb, and opened not my mouth, because
Thou Lord didst it." David's ear was open to hear the
voice of the rod, but his mouth was not open in com-
plaining. Christian, who should you complain of but
yourself? Your own sin has brought you low.

WHAT WE MUST DO WHEN WE ARE BROUGHT LOW

1. Let us search the sin which is the cause of our
trouble. Job 10:2, "Show me wherefore thou contend-
est with me." Lord, what is that sin which has provoked
Thee to bring me low? Lamentations 3:40, "Let us

search and try our ways." As the people of Israel searched the cause when they were worsted in battle, and at last found out the Achan that troubled them and stoned him to death, Joshua 7:18, so let us search out that Achan which has troubled us. Perhaps our sin was censorious. We have been ready to judge and slander others, and now we lie under an evil tongue and have false reports raised on us. Perhaps our sin was pride and God has sent poverty as a thorn to humble us. Perhaps our sin was being remiss in holy duties. We had forgotten our first love and were ready to fall into slumbering fits, and God has sent a sharp cross to awaken us out of our security. We may oftentimes read our sin as our punishment. Oh, let us search the Achan and say as Job, chapter 34:32, "I have done iniquity, I will do so no more."

2. When we are brought low, let us justify God. God is just not only when He punishes the guilty, but when He afflicts the righteous. Let us take heed of entertaining hard thoughts of God, as if He had dealt too severely with us and had put too much wormwood in our cup. No, let us vindicate God and say as the Emperor Mauritius, when he saw five of his sons slain before his eyes by Phocas, "Righteous art Thou, O Lord, in all Thy ways." Let us speak well of God. If we have never so much affliction, yet not one drop of injustice. Psalm 97:2, "Clouds and darkness are round about Him, righteousness and judgment are the habitation of His throne."

3. When we are brought low in affliction, let us bring ourselves low in humiliation. 1 Peter 5:6, "Humble yourselves under the mighty hand of God." When we are in the valley of tears, we must be in the

valley of humility. Lamentations 3:19, "Remembering the wormwood and the gall, my soul hath them continually in remembrance, and is humbled in me." If our condition is low, then it is time to have our hearts lie low.

4. When we are brought low in affliction, let us be on our knees in prayer. Psalm 130:1, "Out of the depths have I cried to Thee, O Lord." Psalm 79:8, "Let Thy tender mercies speedily prevent us, for we are brought very low." Jacob never prayed so fervently as when he was in fear of his life. He oiled the key of prayers with tears. Hosea 12:4, "He wept and made supplication." One reason why God lets us be brought low is to heighten a spirit of prayer.

But what should we pray for in affliction? Let us pray that all our hell may be here. As Pilate said concerning Christ, Luke 23:22, "I will chastise Him and let Him go," so pray that God, when He does chastise us, will let us go, that He will free us from hell and damnation. Let us pray rather for the santification of affliction than the removal of it. Pray that the rod may be a divine pencil to draw God's image more lively upon our souls, Hebrews 12:10, that afflication may be a furnace to refine us, not consume us. Pray that if God does correct us, it may not be in anger, Psalm 6:1, that we may taste the honey of His love at the end of the rod. Let it be our prayer that God will lay no more upon us than He will enable us to bear, 1 Corinthians 10:13, and that if the burden is heavier, our shoulders may be stronger.

5. When we are brought low, let our faith be high. Let us believe that God intends us no harm. Though He casts us into the deep, He will not drown us.

Believe that He is still a Father. He afflicts us in as much mercy as He gives Christ to us. By His rod of discipline, He fits us for the inheritance, Colossians 1:12. Oh, let this star of faith appear in the dark night of affliction. Jonah's faith was never more in heaven than when he lay in the belly of hell, Jonah 2:4.

6. When we are brought low in affliction, let us labor to be bettered by being brought low. Pick some good out of the cross. Get some honey out of this lion. The wicked are worse for affliction. Weeds stamped in a mortar are more unsavory. 2 Chronicles 28:22, "In the time of his distress did he trespass yet more against the Lord. This is that King Ahaz." But let us labor to be meliorated and made better by affliction. Christ learned obedience by what He suffered, Hebrews 5:8. If we are brought low in affliction and get no good, then the affliction is lost.

QUESTION. When are we bettered by affliction?

ANSWER 1. When our eyes are more opened and we are not only chastened but taught, Psalm 94:12. Wormwood is bitter to the taste but is good to clear the eyesight. Our spiritual eyesight is cleared:

1. When we see more of God's holiness. He is a jealous and sin-hating God. He will not suffer evil in His own children to go unpunished. If they make light of sin, He will make their chain heavy, Lamentations 3:2.

2. When we have a clearer insight into ourselves. We see more of our hearts than we did before. We see that earthliness, impatience, and distrust of God which we did not reveal before. We never thought we had such a flux of corruption or that there had been so

much of the old man in the new man. The fire of affliction make that scum of sin boil up which before lay hidden. When our eyesight is thus cleared and both the rod and the lamp go together, now we are bettered by affliction.

ANSWER 2. When our hearts are softened. Affliction is God's furnace where He melts His gold. Jeremiah 9:7, "I will melt them and try them." When our eyes are more watery, our thoughts more serious, our consciences more tender, when we can say as Job, chapter 23:16, "God makes my heart soft." This melting of the heart whereby we are fitted to receive the impression of the Holy Ghost is a blessed sign we are bettered by affliction.

ANSWER 3. When our wills are subdued. Micah 7:9, "I will bear the indignation of the Lord, because I have sinned against Him." Why does God bring us low but to tame our cursed hearts? When a wicked man is brought low, he quarrels with God. Therefore he is compared to a wild bull in a net, Isaiah 51:20. If you go to rub a piece of stuff which is rotten, it frets and tears. So, when God rubs a wicked man by affliction, he frets and tears himself with vexation. Isaiah 8:21, "They shall fret themselves, and curse their King and their God."

But when our spirits are calmed, and we are brought to a sweet submission to God's will, we accept the punishment, Leviticus 26:41, and in patience possess our souls, Luke 21:19. When we say as Eli, 1 Samuel 3:18, "It is the Lord, let Him do what seemeth Him good." I know this trial is in mercy. God would rather afflict me than lose me. Let Him hedge me with thorns if He will plant me with flowers. "Let Him do what seemeth Him good." Now we are bettered by the affliction.

ANSWER 4. When sin is purged out. Isaiah 27:9, "This is all the fruit to take away iniquity." Our hearts are foul and sinful. Our gold is mixed with dross, our stars with clouds. Now, when affliction consumes pride, formality, hypocrisy, when God's lance lets out our spiritual abcess, then we are bettered by affliction.

ANSWER 5. When our hearts are more unglued from the world. What are all these earthly things! The cares of the world exceed the comforts. The emblem that King Henry VII used was a crown of gold hung in a bush of thorns. Many who have escaped the rocks of scandalous sins have been cast away upon the golden sands. The Arabic proverb is, "The world is a carcass, and they who hunt after it are dogs." Has not love of the world become a disease of almost epidemic proportions? If the Lord bestows a plentiful estate upon men, they are apt to make an idol of it. Therefore, God is forced to take that out of their hand which kept Him out of their heart. Now, when the Lord comes and afflicts any of us in that which we love most, He hits us in the apple of our eye and our hearts grow more dead to the world and sick of love to Christ. When God has been withering our gourd and our affections begin to wither, when He has been digging around our root and we are more loosened from the earth, then we are bettered by affliction.

ANSWER 6. When affliction has produced more appetite for the Word. Perhaps in health and prosperity we and the Bible seldom met, or, if we chanced to read, it was but in a dull, cursory manner. But the Lord, by embittering the breast of the creature, has made us run to the breast of a promise. Now we can say with David, Psalm 119:103, "How sweet are Thy words unto my taste; yea, sweeter than honey." Solomon said, "Truly the light is sweet," Ecclesiastes 11:7. But we can say, "Truly the Word is sweet." We have tasted Christ in a promise; the Word has caused an exuberance of joy, Psalm 19:8. This is the manna we love to feed upon. Every leaf of Scripture drops myrrh and, as a rich cordial, cheers our spirit. When it is thus, we are bettered by our trials, Psalm 119:50.

ANSWER 7. When our title to heaven is more confirmed. In prosperity, we are more careless in getting, at least in clearing our spiritual title. People would be loath if their evidences for their land were no better than their evidences for heaven. Many a man's evidence for glory is either forged or blotted. He is not able to read any discriminating work of God's Spirit. He is pendulous and hangs in a doubtful suspense, not knowing whether he has grace or not. Now, when we are brought low by affliction and we fall to the work of self-examination, we see how matters stand between God and our souls. We turn over every leaf of the book of conscience. We make a critical descant upon our hearts and, after a thorough survey of ourselves, we can say, "We know the grace of God in truth," Colossians 1:6. "We have received the holy anointing," 1 John 2:27. Our grace will bear the touchstone, though not the balance. Certainly, then, we have made a good proficiency in the time of affliction and are bettered by it.

ANSWER 8. When we grow more fruitful in grace. A Christian should be like the olive tree, fair and of goodly fruit, Jeremiah 11:16. There is a tree in the Isle of Pomonia which has its fruit folded and wrapped up in the leaves of it, an emblem of a good Christian who has the fruits of grace wrapped up in the leaves of his profession. Now, after pruning, what fruits have we brought forth? The fruits of obedience, love, self-denial, meekness, heavenliness, and longing to be with Christ? If the sharp frost of affliction has brought on the spring flowers of grace, which the Apostle calls the "peaceable fruits of righteousness," Hebrews 12:11, then we are bettered by affliction. A fruitful heart is better than a full crop.

ANSWER 9. When we really commiserate and put on compassion to those who are in a suffering condition. Jesus Christ, having suffered, is touched with our infirmity, Hebrews 4:15. Having felt hunger and cold, He knows how to pity us. Before we have drunk of the bitter cup, instead of pitying others in misery, we are ready to despise them. Psalm 123:4, "Our soul is filled with the scorning of them which are at ease." But when we have been under the harrow and can sympathize with our suffering brethren, and weep with those who weep, this is a sign we are bettered by the affliction. In music, when one string is touched, all the rest sound. So, our "bowels sound as an harp," Isaiah 16:11.

ANSWER 10. When we have learned to bless God in our affliction. Job 1:21, "The Lord hath taken away, blessed be the name of the Lord." Many can bless God when He is giving. Job blessed Him when He took away. This is excellent, not only to praise God when we are upon the mountain of prosperity but in the valley of adversity. Deuteronomy 8:10, "When thou hast eaten and art full, then thou shalt bless the Lord." But it is a greater matter to bless Him when we are empty and in need. 1 Thessalonians 5:18, "In everything give thanks."

QUESTION. But what should we bless God for in
affliction?

ANSWER. We are to bless God that it is no worse
with us. He might have put more gall in our cup, Ezra
9:14. We are to bless God that He will choose rather to
correct us in the world than to condemn us with the
world, 1 Corinthians 11:32. That He has made affliction a means to prevent sin, that He has proportioned
our strength to our trials; that He gives us any support
in our trouble, Psalm 112:4. Though He does not
break our yoke, He lines our yoke with inward peace
and makes it soft and pleasant. We are to bless God
that He deals with us as children, setting His seal of affliction on us and so marking us for His own. We are to
bless God that Christ has taken the sting out of the
cross, that there is a hope of better things laid up for
us in heaven, Colossians 1:5. When we can, upon these
considerations, break forth into a holy gratitude and
triumph in affliction, this is to be bettered by affliction,
and it shows that the Spirit of God and glory rests upon
us, 1 Peter 4:14.

To bless God in heaven when He is crowning us
with glory is no wonder, but to bless God when He is
correcting us, to bless Him in a prison, to give thanks
on a sickebed, not only to kiss the rod but to bless the
hand that holds it, here is the sun in its zenith. This
speaks a very high degree of grace, indeed, and very
much adorns our sufferings.

If we can find these sweet fruits of the cross, we may
assure ourselves that the affliction is sanctified. We may
say with David, Psalm 119:71, "It is good for me that I
was afflicted." And then God will throw away the rod
and will make us glad after the days of our mourning.

Ezekiel 16:42, "So will I make my fury towards thee to rest, and My jealousy shall depart from thee, and I will be quiet and will be no more angry."

BRANCH 3. If sin brings us low, let us labor to bring our sins low. Let all our spite be at sin. Let us pursue it with a holy malice. Sin has brought us even to the dust and would bring us lower into the abyss of hell. Let us then shed the blood of sin which would shed our blood. Colossians 3:5, "Mortify your members which are upon the earth, fornication, uncleanness, etc."

We are apt to plead for sin, "Is it not a little one?" Who would plead for the one who seeks his life? We are ready to say to the minister concerning sin, as David said to Joab concerning Absalom, 2 Samuel 18:5, "Deal gently with the young man." So, we are ready to say, "Sir, deal gently with my sins. Oh, do not be too sharp in your reproofs!"

Why not? Does not the traitor sin and seek to take away your crown of glory, as Absalom did his father's crown? Would it not bring you low? If, therefore, you are wise, do not spare it. Do with your sin as Joab did with Absalom. He took three darts in his hand and thrust them through the heart of Absalom, 2 Samuel 18:14. So take these three darts—the Word of God, prayer, and mortification—and strike through the heart of your lusts so that they die. Do as Sampson did in dealing with the Philistines. They brought him low, put out his eyes, and he never left till he was revenged on them and brought them low. Judges 16:30, "He bowed himself with all his might, and the house fell upon the Lords." Sampson died, but we live by the

death of our enemies. Oh, that every day some limb of
the old man may drop off!

What is the end of all a Christian's duties, praying,
and hearing, but to weaken and mortify lust? Why is
this spiritual medicine taken but to kill the child of sin?
Sin will insinuate itself and plead for a reprieve, but
show it no mercy. Saul's sparing Agag lost him the
kingdom, and your sparing sin will lose you the kingdom of heaven.

BRANCH 4. Last, let this make us weary of living in
the world, for while we live in sin, sin brings us low. We
eat the forbidden fruit and then are sick afterwards.
How should this make us to long to have our pass to be
gone and cry, "Oh, that we had the wings of a dove, to
fly away and be at rest!" Then we shall shake off those
vipers which leaped upon us. 1 Corinthians 3:22,
"Death is yours." At death, we shall have an eternal ju-
bilee and be freed from all encumbrances.

Sin shall be no more. Death smites a believer as the
angel smote Peter on his side and made his chains fall
off, Acts 12:7. So death smites a believer and makes the
chains of his sins fall off.

Trouble shall be no more. This lower region is full
of storms. Troubles and vexations are some of the
thorns with which the earth is cursed. But in the grave,
a believer has his quiet place. "There the wicked cease
from troubling, there the weary are at rest," Job 3:17.
God will shortly wipe away all tears, Revelation 7:17.
How this should make the saints desire to be dissolved,
Philippians 1:23! Israel's being so often stung with serpents made them weary of the wilderness and aspire after Canaan. The discourtesies a prince meets with in a

strange land make him long to be in his own country where the royal crown will be set upon his head. When we are with Christ, we shall be brought low no more. We shall never be fixed stars till we are in heaven.

Oh, the felicity of glorified saints! They have a full-eyed vision of God and those refulgent beams of glory are darted from His blessed face and delight, yea, ravish their hearts with ineffable joy. The birds of the fortunate islands are nourished with perfumes. After death, the saints shall be forever nourished with the aromatics and perfumes of their Saviour's love.

2

The Desperateness
of Sinners
They Sin Still.

"For all this, they sinned still."
Psalm 78:32

The people of Israel were called by God's name.
They were selected from all the people of the earth.
Deuteronomy 7:6, "The Lord thy God hath chosen
thee, to be a special people unto Himself, above all the
people that are upon the face of the earth." The other
part of the world was but rubbish; these were jewels.
The other was forest ground; these are God's enclosure. Exodus 19:6, "Ye shall be unto me a Kingdom of
priests." But even Israel had a blot on their name-plate.
The text draws up a black charge against them, "For all
this, they sinned still."

For all what? God had been very good to Israel. He
had bestowed many favors on them. Verse 13, "He divided the sea." He made a highway for them there, and
made the waters to be as walls on each side of them.
Verse 14, "In the day time, He led them with a cloud."
This was a special figure of God's protection. The pil-

lar of cloud was to conduct them and keep off the scorching heat of the sin. The pillar of fire was to be their torch to light them by night. Verse 24, "He rained down manna upon them to eat." It was called angel's food for the excellence of it, such as the angels might have eaten if they ate food. Israel had the cream of God's blessings, but for all this, they sinned still.

Then, God inflicted punishment on them. After the sunshine of mercy came thunder. Verse 31, "The wrath of God came upon them." In the Hebrew it is, "It ascended as a flame." What this wrath was is specified in verse 19, "He sent evil angels among them." They were evil in the effect. They smote the people with pestilence. Yet, "for all this, they sinned still."

This showed the bad temper of this people. They were worse for all the medicines God had used for their healing. "They sinned still."

The text divides itself into three parts:

1. Israel's crime: They sinned.
2. The aggravation of their sin: For all this.
3. Their continuance in sin: They sinned still.

DOCTRINE: None of God's dealings with the wicked will prevail with them to break off their sins. "For all this, they sinned still."

To sin still is, first, heinous, because it shows a contempt of God. Let God say what He will, yet men go on in sin. This is to condemn God and bid Him do His worst. Psalm 10:3, "Wherefore doth the wicked condemn God?"

To sin still is, second, desperate, because it is to sin against the remedy. If no means God uses will prevail, persons are incurable. If a member is cut off, yet the body gangrenes. There is no help for the patient and he must die. If nothing will do the sinner good and he still continues in sin, this man's case is past hope. There is no way but hell.

USE 1. OF INFORMATION

BRANCH 1. I note hence the blindness of every sinner. He does not see that evil in sin which should make him leave it. He sins still. To this day, the veil is upon his heart. Sin is the spirit and quintessence of evil, but the unregenerate person is enveloped with ignorance. If he dies in sin, he is damned irrecoverably. But he sports with his own damnation—he sins still. Sin has made him not only sick but senseless. Though sin has death and hell following it, yet he is so blind that he sins still.

We pity blind men. How is every graceless man to be pitied whom the god of this world has blinded, 2 Corinthians 4:4? The devil carries a wicked man as the falconer does the hawk, hoodwinked to hell. But he does not see the danger he is in. He is like a bird that hastens to the snare and does not see the snare.

BRANCH 2. See hence the love and amity between man's heart and sin. "They sinned still." Sin is a dish men cannot forbear. Hosea 13:1, "Who look to other gods and love flagons of wine." Psalm 4:2, "How long will ye love vanity?" The heart and sin are like two lovers who cannot endure to be parted. A sinner is the greatest self-denier. For the love of sin, he will deny himself a part in heaven. One would think, "There is so little in sin, why should it be loved?" Who would

pour rose water into a sink? Who would spend so sweet
an affection as love upon so filthy a thing as sin?

Sin is a thorn in the conscience. It is a sword in the
bones. Psalm 38:3, "I have no rest in my bones, because
of my sin." Whatever deflowers, disturbs. Yet such is the
love that a man bears to his sin that he will venture all
for his lusts —the loss of God's favor and the loss of his
soul.

BRANCH 3. See the desperate obstinance of sinners; they persist in sin contumaciously. "They sinned
still." Though God has pronounced a blessing and a
curse (a blessing upon those who forsake sin, a curse
upon those who continue in sin), yet they choose the
curse over the blessing. The wicked are pertinacious
and resolved. "They sinned still." The heart of man by
nature is like a garrison which holds out in war.
Though articles of peace are offered, though it is
straightly besieged and one bullet after another is shot,
yet the garrison holds out. So the heart is a garrison
that holds out against God. Though He uses entreaties,
gives warnings, shoots bullets into the conscience, yet
the garrison of the heart holds out. The man will not
be reclaimed; he sins still. He is said to have a brow of
brass, in regard to his impudence, and a sinew of iron,
in regard to his obstinance, Isaiah 48:4.

The sinner is not reformed by all God's judgments.
We see metal that melts in the furnace, but take it out
and it returns to its wonted hardness. The Lord sent
one judgment after another on Pharaoh, and though
he seemed to be melted (Exodus 9:27, "I have sinned,
the Lord is righteous"), yet no sooner was he taken out
of the fire and the plague removed but he sinned still.

Verse 34, "He sinned yet more and hardened his heart."

Some men, in a fit of sickness, when their consciences are so far awakened as to be brought to a sight of hell, and they begin to smell the fire and brimstone, O what promises they make if only God will spare their lives! But, when they recover, they are worse then ever before. They sin still. Isaiah 9:13, "The people turneth not unto Him that smiteth them." Amos 4:6, "I have given you cleanness of teeth." Verse 7, "I have withholden the rain." Verse 10, "I have smitted you with pestilence, yet ye have not returned unto Me, saith the Lord."

What sin do we have left after all God's judgments which have been upon us? Can we show the head of that Goliath lust which is slain? There is so much atheism and hard-heartedness in men, so close an adherence of lust to their souls, that they will go on in sin inflexibly till God, by a miraculous power, stops their course, as He did Paul when he was going with letters to Damascus, Acts 9:2. Oh, the vile obstinance of men—they sin still. Though they are sometimes convinced that they are in a bad way, yet their corruptions are stronger than their convictions. If a wicked man could be fetched out of hell and brought back into a capacity of mercy, yet he would in a second life follow his lusts and sin himself into hell again.

BRANCH 4. I note how hard it will be for such persons to be savingly wrought upon who go on sinning. At first the heart is more tender and fearful of evil. But by keeping up the trade of sin, it is deadened and seared. By sinning still, a man is brought to such a pass that he despises the Word and resists the Spirit.

Reason and conscience are bound like prisoners with the chains of lust. By sinning still, men have contracted a custom of evil. Jeremiah 13:23, "Can the Ethiopian change his skin or the leopard his spots?" Custom in sin stupifies conscience. 'Tis like a gravestone laid upon a man. Oh, how hard their conversion who go on still in their trespasses! That tree will hardly be plucked up which has been long rooting in the earth. How hard will they find it to be plucked up out of their natural estate who have been many years rooting in sin! He who had been possessed with the devil from his youth up found it more hard to have the devil cast out of him, Mark 9:21.

BRANCH 5. See the reason why men's prayers are not heard. It is because they sin still. Sin clips the wings of prayer so that it will not fly to the throne of grace. Psalm 66:18, "If I regard iniquity in my heart, the Lord will not hear me." In the original it is, "If I look upon sin" so as to lust after it. Suppose a man had never so sweet a breath; yet, if he had the plague, you would not come near him. A sinner may give God many a sweet expression in prayer, but the plague sores still break out in his life. He sins still. Therefore, God will not come near to take a petition from him. Malachi 1:10, "I have no pleasure in you, saith the Lord of Hosts, neither will I accept an offering at your hand."

Sin makes the heart hard and God's ear deaf. Men pray, "Lord, have mercy on us; Christ, have mercy on us." But, though they pray still, they sin still. Therefore, God hears their sins and not their prayers. The Lord loves the mourning of His doves but counts the prayers of the wicked no better than the howling of a dog. Hosea 7:14, "They have not cried to Me with their heart when they howled upon their bed." Prayer is a sovereign plaster for a wounded soul, but sin pulls off the plaster so that it will not heal.

The prayers of the wicked put God in mind of their sins and makes Him more speedy in His process of justice against them. Hosea 8:12-13, "I have written to him the great things of My law, but they were counted a strange thing; they sacrifice flesh for My offerings, but the Lord accepteth them not, now will He remember their iniquity and visit their sins." Their sacrificing put God in mind of their sin: "now will He remember their iniquity."

BRANCH 6. See the reason why we suffer still, because we sin still. Jeremiah 8:15, "We looked for peace, but no good came." We expected golden days. There was hope of a spirit of moderation, but fiery comets appear. We sin still. Therefore, God's hand is stretched out still, Isaiah 9:12. Oh, to what a heighth is wickedness boiled up! There are sins in the nation not to be named. Ezekiel 24:13, "In their filthiness is lewdness." We pour on the oil of sin; therefore God's anger still flames. There are still fears upon us, still a consumption in the body politic, still new gripings in the bowels. While the Ephah of sin fills, the vial of wrath fills. We sin still. Therefore, we are still under the black rod.

BRANCH 7. See our unhappiness in a lapsed state. Being fallen from God, we go further and further from Him. "They sinned still." Every sin sets one a step further from God. Jeremiah 2:5, "They are gone far from

Me." How far are they from God who have been all
their lives wandering from Him? Psalm 58:3, "They
wicked are estranged from the womb, they go astray as
soon as they be born." To sin yet still is to take our
farewell of God and go with the Prodigal into the far
country, Luke 15:13. The further one goes from the
sun, the nearer he approaches to darkness; the further
the soul deviates from God, the nearer it approaches to
misery.

BRANCH 8. Note hence how vain are all resolu-
tions to leave sin and be converted until God changes
the heart. "They sinned still." Many think to themselves, "Well, now they will become new men; they will
never do as before; they will be drunk no more; they
will be unclean no more." Alas, they have wind and
tide to carry them to hell and, when they are once sinning, they know not where they shall stop."
    "They sinned still." Let God's afflicting hand lie
upon men, though their strength to sin is abated, yet
not their appetite. When they grow old, their lusts
grow young. Unless the daystar of grace arises in their
hearts and alters their course, they will never leave sinning till they have sinned themselves to the devil. A
bowl running down hill seldom stops in the middle.

BRANCH 9. See the exact notice God takes of
men's impieties. "They sinned still." God observed, and
His pen was going in heaven all the while. People,
through atheism, think surely the Lord does not see
their sins, nor will He call them to account. Psalm
10:11, "He hath said in his heart, God hath forgotten,
He hideth His face, He will never see it." But God takes

a full inspection into men's actions. Jeremiah 16:17, "Mine eyes are upon all their ways, they are not hid from My face."

God takes notice of the aggravations of sin against knowledge, mercy, and example. To God, the world is a *corpus diaphanum*, a clear, transparent body. He sees curtain wickedness. He beholds all the sinful workings of men's hearts like we can see the bees working in their combs in a transparent hive. Matthew 6:4, "He seeth in secret." God observes how long a person persists in wickedness—"they sinned still."

As a merchant keeps his book of accounts and enters debts down in his book, so God has His diary or daybook, and He enters down every sin into the book. Psalm 49:9, "He that formed the eye, shall He not see?" The clouds cannot be a canopy, or the night a dark lantern to hinder His sight. I think this should be a counterpoison against sin. God's eye is never off us. He makes a critical descant upon our actions. We may deceive men, but we cannot deceive our Judge. Ecclesiastes 12:14, "God will bring into judgment every evil thing."

BRANCH 10. See the difference between the wicked and the godly. Nothing can make a wicked man leave off being evil. He sins still. And nothing can make a godly man leave off being good; he is godly still. Though there may be death-threatening times, he will pray still and love God still. Daniel invoked his God, though for all he knew a prayer might cost him his life, Daniel 6:10. Let the waters be never so salty, the fish will still keep their freshness. Genesis 7:11, "Noah was upright in his generation." When all flesh

had corrupted itself, Noah held on to a course of piety.
A godly man will still be godly, whatever he suffers.
Psalm 44:17, "All this is come upon us, yet have we not
forsaken Thee, nor dealt falsely in Thy covenant."

Justum & tenacem proposuit virum,
Nec civium ardor Prava jubentium,
Non vultus Tyranni,
Mente quatit solida.   Horace

He portrayed an upright and steady man;
Neither the frenzy of citizens calling for evil things,
Nor the visage of the tyrant.
Shake him in his firmness of mind.

Gold, though cast in the fire, retains its purity. Acts
20:23, "Bonds and afflictions abide me, but none of
these things move me, neither do I count my life dear."
Though the archers shoot at a godly man, yet the bow
of his faith abides in strength. Whatever he loses, he
holds fast the jewel of a good conscience. He knows
the crown of religion is constancy. And though persecution brings death in one hand, it brings life in the
other. Though religion may have thorns strewn in the
way, the thorns cannot be as sharp as the crown is
sweet.

BRANCH 11. See from hence how provoking it is to
the holy and jealous God to persist in wickedness.
"They sinned still." God speaks as if He were very angry. To sin once may be out of ignorance, and when a
man comes to know it he repents. Or he repents out of
passion, and when the passion is over he weeps. But to

sin still highly incenses God and calls aloud for vengeance. Jeremiah 9:3, "They proceed from evil to evil." Verse 9, "Shall I not visit for these things?"

Every sin is treason against the crown of heaven. Now, the more treasons a person commits, the more he enrages his prince. To sin still is to dare God's justice; 'tis to affront Him to His face, and an affront will make God draw His sword.

Is not this spot upon us? Are there not those among us who habituate themselves to evil and contumaciously persist in their impieties? Shall not God visit for these things? Surely England's furnace is heating, and we may sadly suspect God has some other judgments to bring up the rear. Either God will make us weary of our sins or weary of our lives.

BRANCH 12. See here the nature of sin. One sin makes way for more. "They sinned still." The more they sinned, the more fit they were to sin. It is a curse upon sin that one act prepares for more. Acts 13:2, "And now they sin more and more." In the Hebrew it is "they add to sin." When Jereboam had left off sacrificing to the true God, he did not stop there but set up golden calves at Dan and Bethel for the people to worship, 1 Kings 12:29. Absalom prevaricated with his father and made religion an excuse for his lie. This sin prepared him for treason, 2 Samuel 15:10. Peter's denial of Christ was seconded with an oath, and that oath backed with a curse. Matthew 26:74, "Then began he to curse." Some think he cursed Christ. Cain first envied his brother. Then envy begat anger and anger begat murder. One sin draws on more. If you let a little water out of a pipe it makes way for more. Oh, how

dangerous is it to give way to one sin! One sin leads the
van, and whole troops follow. "They sinned still." When
acts of sin are multiplied, men go to hell and never
stop.

BRANCH 13. See the patience of God towards
men. They sinned still, yet God bore with them and,
many times, deferred judgment. Psalm 78:38, "Many a
time turned He His anger away." How long did God
bear with the old world? He strives with men by His
Word and Spirit. He comes to them in a still voice. He
would win them with His love. "He waiteth to be gracious," Isaiah 30:18. God is not like a hasty creditor
who requires the debt and will give no time for the
payment. Revelation 2:21, "I gave her space to repent."
The Lord blows the trumpet a long time before His
murdering piece. The wicked sin still and God is patient still. 2 Peter 3:9, "He is long-suffering to usward,
not willing that any should perish."
Justice says, "Cut them down."
Patience says, "Spare them a year longer."
When God is going to strike, He repents and stays
so long till He is weary of repenting, as the Prophet
speaks, Jeremiah 15:6.
We of this nation spin out our sins and God is yet
patient. But He will not always be so. If we go on impa-
tiently, the lease of patience will at last be run out. And
the longer God is saving His blow, the heavier it will
be.
God's patience has bounds and landmarks set to it.
There is a time when God will say, "My Spirit shall no
longer strive," Revelation 14:7. The angel cried, "The
hour of God's judgment is come," Ezekiel 30:3. Sodom

was the wonder of God's patience, but now has been made a monument of His anger. The Lord may keep off the stroke a long time, but if men are unreclaimable and sin still, let them know that vengeance is not dead but sleeping. Sins against patience exceed the sins of the fallen angels. Therefore, the fiery furnace will be heated seven times hotter.

BRANCH 14. See here that which will justify God in damning the wicked: They sinned still. Oh, how righteous God will be when He shall pass the sentence against them! When a thief goes on stealing and, after he has been reprieved he still robs, how will all applaud the judge in condemning him! Wicked men are now ready to charge God with paritality and injustice. Ezekiel 18:25, "Ye have said, The way of the Lord is not equal." They think it very hard that they should die for eating the apple of pleasure. But God will say, "Did I not forbid you that fruit? Yet you ate it; nay, you continued eating it. You sinned still. What can you say for yourselves as to why you should not die?"

Sinners will be found speechless. Psalm 51:4, "That Thou mayest be clear when Thou judgest." A wicked man will, at the last day, clear God of all injustice. It is a great vindication of a judge when the prisoner at the bar shall, in the face of the country, clear his judge and acknowledge that the sentence of death is righteous. Every wicked man's conscience shall set this seal to the righteousness of God's judgment.

BRANCH 15. See what a powerful thing grace is, that gives check to corruption and breaks the heart off from the love of sin. Though a gracious soul has sin in him, yet he cannot be said properly to sin still, 1 John 3:9. He does not allow himself in sin, Romans 7:15. He maintains a combat with it, Galatians 5:17. Though he may fall into sin, he does not lie in it. A sheep may fall into the dirt, but does not lie there. In this sense, a child of God is said to be dead to sin, Romans 6:2. Oh, how mighty and sovereign is divine grace, which divorces a person from sin!

If you consider what power sin has in a man, it is a miracle that he should forsake it. Sin is a man's self, like a member of the body which is not easily parted with. Sin is woven and incorporated into the nature of a man. It is as natural to sin as for fire to burn. Sin has bewitched and stolen away the heart. Now, that sin which has gotten such power over a man should be beaten out of all its forts and castles, what a wonder this is! How is it but from invincible grace? The Spirit draws sweetly but irresistibly. It allures yet conquers. Grace sits paramount in the soul. It is that strong water which eats asunder the iron chain of sin. Grace repels and beats back corruption. Psalm 114:5, "What ailed thee, O thou sea, that thou fledst? Thou, Jordan, that thou wast driven back?"

So, in a man who before was under the command of corruption, at last sin flies and is driven back. What ails this man? Behold the power of omnipotent grace that has made such a sudden alteration in him. It has routed sin's forces and caused this Jordan to be driven back.

BRANCH 16. See the sordid ingratitude of sinners. "They sinned still." Notwithstanding the fact that they had such eminent and signal favors from God—the pillar of fire to lead them, the rock split to give them water—yet mercy could not, with all its oratory, prevail with them to leave their iniquities. "They sinned still."

A father bribes his son to obedience by giving him money, yet he still goes on in dissolute courses. So God would draw men from sin by His mercies, yet they will indulge their sensual appetite. Oh, ungrateful! It is an ill nature that will not be won with love. Beasts are wrought upon with kindness, Isaiah 1:3, but sinners are not. The wicked are worse for mercies. They, like vultures, draw sickness from these perfumes.

The wicked deal with God as we do with the Thames. The Thames brings us in our riches—our gold, silks, and spices—and we throw all our filth into the Thames. Just so do the wicked deal with God. He gives them all their mercies and they commit their filthy sins against Him. "They sinned still." Ingratitude is, as St. Bernard said, the enemy of salvation. If mercy is not a magnet to draw us nearer to God, it will be a millstone to sink us deeper into hell. Nothing so cold as lead, yet nothing more scalding when it is melted. Nothing so sweet as mercy, yet nothing so terrible when it is abused. Sinners never escape when mercy draws up their indictment.

BRANCH 17. See the egregious folly of sinners. "They sinned still." Though they had felt the smart of sin, verse 21, a fire was kindled in Jacob and anger came up against Israel. Yet for all this, they sinned still. This viper of sin had pained them, yet they put it in their bosom again. Sin has done all the spite to men that it can. It has exhausted their health; it has brought them to a prison and almost to hell, yet they sin still.

While the bears lick the honey around the hive, they are stung with the bees. So, for that little pleasure in sin, men's consciences are stung and in torment, yet they sin still. They would be angry to have others call them fools, but the Scripture does, Proverbs 14:9. Nay, the time is coming when they will call themselves fools. Provers 11:12, "And thou mourn at last saying, How have I hated instruction!" What, to love those cords that bound me? How foolish I was! "How have I hated instruction!"

BRANCH 18. See what vast treasures of wrath are laid up for sinners, Romans 2:4. "They sinned still." As guilt increases, so does wrath. Every sin committed is a stick to heat hell and make it burn the hotter. It is a thing to be lamented that men should live in the world only to increase their torments in hell. While they commit new sins, they are burdening themselves with more irons, which will be so heavy at last they will not know how to bear them or avoid them. "They sinned still."

Oh, sinner! Know that for every lie you tell, every oath you swear, you are only adding to your torment! Every dish Satan serves in will increase your fatal reckoning. Every time you defraud others and make your weights lighter, you make your condemnation heavier. Every sin is a drop of oil upon hell's flame.

BRANCH 19. See what cause they have to admire the stupendous goodness of God who has wrought a change in them, and checked them in their full career of sin. Matthew 11:26, "Even so, Father, for it seemeth good in Thy sight." Christians, you who are vessels of election, were by nature as wicked as others, but God had compassion on you and plucked you as brands out of the fire. He stopped you in your course of sinning, perhaps by an arrow shot out of a pulpit, perhaps by setting a thornhedge of affliction in your way. Even as the angel stood in the way to stop Balaam when he was riding on, Numbers 22:31, so God stood in your way and stopped you when you were marching to hell. He turned you back to Him by repentance. Oh, here is the banner of love displayed over you! 1 Timothy 1:13, "Who was a blasphemer and a persecutor, but I obtained mercy." Literally, I was "bemercied."

Christians, why might not you have been in the number of those who sin still? Who at their dice use this litany, "Devil help me, God damn me." Why might not you have been Sabbath breakers or persecutors? But God has bemiracled you with mercy.

Behold, distinguishing grace. Let your hearts melt in love to God. Admire His royal bounty. Celebrate the memorial of His goodness. Set the crown of all your praises upon the head of free grace.

BRANCH 20. Last, I note from this how agreeable to reason it is that God should damn men eternally for sin—not only because sin is acted against an infinite majesty, but because there is an eternity of sin in men's nature. "They sinned still." Should men live forever, they would sin forever. Some think it hard that for the sins committed in a few years they should undergo perpetual torment, but here lies the justice and equity of it. It is because sinners have an everlasting principle of sin in them. Their stock of corruption would never be quite spent. They have a never-dying appetite to sin, which is justly punished with a never-dying worm.

USE 2. OF REPROOF

It serves to reprove such as sin yet still. He who was unclean is unclean still; he who was drunk is drunk still. Hosea 7:10, "They do not return to the Lord." Jeremiah 9:3, "They proceed from evil to evil." Psalm 78:17, "They sinned yet more against Him."

And let me not only speak to scandalous sinners, who seem to have damnation written upon their foreheads, but to secret sinners. Deuteronomy 27:15, "Cursed be he that makes an idol and puts it in a secret place." Some of the Jews would not be seen openly bowing to an idol, but they would put it in their closet or some other place and there worship it. There are many in like manner who will not sin on the balcony, or be like Absalom and sin in the sight of all Israel, 2 Samuel 16:22 (that would be to call the devil "Father" out loud), but they shut up their shop windows and follow their trade within doors. They carry their sins cunningly. They have a private back door to hell which nobody knows of. Perhaps they live in secret adultery or secret envy and malice or secret neglect of duty. God and men's consciences know whether they are guilty of living in secret sins. But to such as sin still, whether more openly or secretly, consider what an aggravation of sin this is.

God's watchmen have been sent to warn men of their evil ways. They have told them how damnable a thing it is to persist in sin. The judgments of God, like arrows, have been shot at them for sin. Yet for all this, they sin still. This is worse than to be Balaam the Sorcerer. For when he saw the angel before him with a naked sword, he dared not ride on. But these desperate, heaven-daring sinners, though they see the flaming sword of God's justice before them, resolvedly venture on in sin.

This sin is willful. Willful disobeyers are said to reproach the Lord, Numbers 15:30. To defy a prince's authority is to reproach him. Willfulness in sin amounts to presumption. Psalm 19:13, "Keep back Thy servant from presumptuous sins." Under the Law, there were sacrifices for sins of ignorance, but no sacrifices for sins of presumption, Numbers 11:30. To sin willfully accents and enhances the sin. It is like die to the wool or like a weight put in the scale which makes it weigh heavier. This leaves men without excuse, John 15:22. If a sea mark is set up to give notice that there are shelves or rockes, the mariner still will sail there. If he splits his ship, no one will pity him because he had warning given.

Pilate sinned desperately. He knew the Jews had arraigned Christ out of envy, Matthew 27:18. He confessed that he found no fault in Him, Luke 23:14. And God went about to stop him in his sin. He admonished him through his wife's telling him to have nothing to do with that just man, Matthew 27:19. Yet for all this, he went on and gave sentence against Christ. While Pilate condemned Christ, he himself was condemned by his own conscience.

Add but one degree of sin more to presumption, spiting the Spirit, and it becomes the unpardonable sin. When men sin and will sin, it is just with God to harden them and leave them to themselves. Seeing they will be filthy, let them be filthy still, Revelation 22:11. That is a heart-saddening text in Hosea 8:11, "Because Ephraim hath made many altars to sin, altars shall be unto him for sin." 'Tis dreadful for a man to be left to himself, like a ship without a rudder or pilot driven out of the winds and dashed upon a rock. Roman 1:24, "Wherefore also God gave them up to uncleanness."

What is the condition of a patient when his physician gives him over and leaves him to his own sick palate? The physcian is saying, "Medicine will do him no good; you may let him eat what he pleases, for he will die."

USE 3. OF EXHORTATION

Let it exhort all to take heed of Israel's disease of sinning still. John 5:14, "Sin no more, lest a worse thing come unto thee." Oh, sinners, if Christ, glory, or salvation is of any value to you, hearken to this sacred charm of the gospel, and be entreated to "break off your iniquities by righteousness," Daniel 4:27. 'Tis not arbitrary, but lies upon you by virtue of a solemn command. Job 22:23, "Thou shalt put away iniquity, far from thy tabernacles." The Hebrew word there signifies to put away sin with indignation, like Paul shook off the viper. Either you must put your sin far away or God will put you far away. It is sad that a man should be so far bewitched with the woman's hair that he does not read the lion's teeth, Revelation 9:7. Oh, break off a course of impiety!

Let your hearts be cleansed from the love of sin. Grace begins with the heart. Jeremiah 4:14, "Wash thy

heart, O Jerusalem." Wash in holy tears. The salt water
of tears kills the worm of conscience. To go to cleanse
the life before the heart is cleansed is as if you should
wash the channel when the fountain is polluted.

Enter upon a new course of life. Jeremiah 7:3,
"Amend your ways and your doings." In the Hebrew it
is, "Make good your ways."

OBJECTION. But we have no power of ourselves to
put a stop to sin. We cannot convert ourselves.

ANSWER. Do what you can. Men are not mere logs;
they may do more than they do. They may avoid the
occasions of sin. They may put themselves upon the
use of means. They may lie at the pool of an ordinance
and there wait for the angels to stir the water. Those
feet which will carry them to a tavern or play will carry
them to a sermon. They may implore God in prayer to
enable them to break off sin. God, who sometimes
meets those who are running from Him, will not despise those who run to Him. There is a promise on
record, Jeremiah 29:13, "Then shall ye find Me, when
ye search for Me with all your heart." Go to God, then,
and He will give grace. God no sooner speaks than He
creates. When God speaks, the heart opens to Him like
the flower opens with the sun.

Poor sinners, if you see yourselves lost and seek
Christ, while you are seeking Him, He is seeking you,
Luke 19:10. And to encourage you in your earnest addresses to God, remember that God has made a
promise not only to those who have grace, but to those
who lack it. Proverbs 1:23, "Turn you at My reproof,
behold I will pour out My Spirit upon you." Pray over
this promise and, in due time, God will infuse His

Spirit which shall work that in you which He requires
of you.

SOME MOTIVES TO DIVORCE SIN

Having answered this objection, let me use some
few prevalent motives to persuade men to put a bill of
divorce in the hand of their sins.

1. *Consider that, while men go on still in sin, God is their
professed Enemy, and He will raise all the force and militia of
heaven against them.* Psalm 68:21, "God shall wound the
hairy scalp of such an one as goeth on still in his trespasses." A wound that touches the brain is mortal. All
God's bearded arrows fly among the wicked. 'Tis dangerous to stand in the place where God's arrows fly.
Perhaps, some may think, God's wrath is not so terrible. The lion is not as fierce as he is painted. Consult
that text, Deuteronomy 32:41, "If I whet My glittering
sword, I will render vengeance to Mine enemies, I will
make My arrows drunk with blood."

Oh, sinner, who still wallows in your swinish filthiness, do you know what an enemy you have in the
field? It is He who stretches out the heavens and laid
the foundations of the earth, Isaiah 51:13, who rebukes
the wind and bridles the sea. It is He who can look you
into your grave, who can bind you in chains among the
devils; and will you go on to provoke Him? Can you
make your part good with God? "Hast thou an arm like
God?" Job 40:9. Can a child grapple with a giant or an
arch-angel? Ezekiel 22:14, "Can thy heart endure, or
thy hands be strong in the day that I shall deal with
thee?"

Sinner, you have done enough to damn your soul already, and God has you at an advantage every hour; but there is yet a white flag of mercy held forth. You may yet make your peace with God. And there is no way to appease God but by the death of your sins. Oh, then, make haste. Bring to God the head of your beloved sin on a plate. There is no pacification but by mortification.

2. *What is there in sin that anyone should persist in it?* It is the spirit of mischief; it is a breach of the royal law, 1 John 3:4. It defaces God's image in the soul; it is like a stain to beauty; it is the matter of which the worm of conscience breeds; it is properly the work of the devil. 1 John 3:8, "The devil sins from the beginning." And is there no other employment a man can busy himself about but the work of the devil? Sin ushers in death, Romans 6:22. Do not say that it is sweet. What wise man would drink poison because it is sweet? Who would desire a pleasure that kills?

3. *The great benefit which accrues to a person by breaking off sin.* Sinner, the day you leave your sins and set upon a course of holiness, God will pardon all that is past. It shall be as if you had never offended. God will pass an act of oblivion. Jeremiah 31:34, "I will remember your sins no more." The Lord never upbraids a penitent with former unkindnesses.

OBJECTION. But may the sinner say, "I am so loaded with guilt that I fear there is no hope of mercy for me?"

ANSWER 1. Though you are guilty, and conscience, like God's attorney, charges you with a foul libel of

particular sins, yet, if you are truly humbled and
bruised in the sight of God, know that your case is not
desperate. 1 John 2:1, "If any man sin, we have an advocate with the Father, Jesus Christ the Righteous."

Nay, Christ is not only an Advocate but a Surety,
Hebrews 7:22. And, though you are even drowned in
debt, yet Christ, by His merit, has satisfied justice and
brought in everlasting righteousness for you, Daniel
9:24. Wait but awhile and He will, in due time, give to
your conscience a full discharge sealed with the testi-
mony of His own Spirit.

ANSWER 2. All winds of providence shall blow you
to heaven. Romans 8:28, "All things work together for
good." You shall be a gainer by your losses. Your
crosses shall be turned into blessings. Poverty shall
starve your lusts. Sickness shall refine your grace.
Persecution shall bring you nearer to God. All the
stones the Jews threw at Stephen knocked him faster to
Christ the Cornerstone, Isaiah 28:16. Every cut of
God's spiritual diamonds makes them sparkle the
more. Afflictions are not so much to wound the godly
as to warn them. They are not the blows of an enemy,
but the tokens of a Father. God will sugar every affliction with His love. The people of God gather grapes of
thorns. It is a great controversy between the chemists
and the physicians whether gold may be made liquid
and drunk as a cordial. I am sure that, to the people of
God, afflictions become gold and, being drunk down,
they have been cordial and cheering to their hearts. 2
Corinthians 1:5, "As the sufferings of Christ abound in
us, so our consolation also aboundeth."

ANSWER 3. God will display the banner of free
grace over you. He will smile on you, embrace you in

the arms of His mercy, and kiss you with the kisses of His lips. He will lead you into the banqueting house and feast you with those royal dainties and rare foods with which the angels are delighted. He will give you the hidden manna and the wine of paradise. He will bestow on you "change of raiment and set the fair mitre" of glory on your head, Zechariah 3:4-5.

In short, God will say to you, as Pharaoh said to Joseph, Genesis 45:20, "The good of all the land is yours." So, the whole kingdom is before you; the good of that heavenly land is yours; and, as the father of the repenting Prodigal said, Luke 15:21, "Son, all I have is thine." My power is yours to help you. My Spirit is yours to comfort you. My mercy is yours to save you. All I have is yours. I give you not only My jewels, but Myself, and what more can I give you?

Oh, therefore, all you sinners, be persuaded to put a stop to your sins. Do it sincerely, Jeremiah 24:7. Hypocrisy in religion will damn as well as profaneness. Do it speedily, Jeremiah 18:11. Death may be within a few day's march of you. But part with your lusts and "this day is salvation come to your house."

OBJECTION. But suppose a few of us break off a course of sinning? What are we the better if the greatest part of the people go on sinning still? Wrath is likely to come upon the land?

ANSWER 1. Yet if you cannot save the kingdom, you may save your own souls. And a soul saved is more than a world gained.

ANSWER 2. Perhaps the reformation of a few may help to keep off wrath from the nation. Jeremiah 5:1, "Run ye to and fro, and see now if ye can find a man

that seeketh the truth, and I will pardon it." God would
have spared Sodom for ten righteous men, but here
He comes lower. If there were but one righteous man,
He would pardon. The people of Jerusalem were generally so corrupt that one might have gone up and
down the streets in it and scarcely found a man who
was sincerely righteous. But if by this word "man" we
understand "few," yet that shows us that sometimes the
repentance of a few may help to save a nation. A few
ears of good corn may save a whole field of tares from
being plucked up.

ANSWER 3. Perhaps, if desolating judgments
should come upon others, God may spare you.
Zephaniah 2:3, "Seek righteousness, it may be ye shall
be hid in the day of the Lord's anger." The Lord knows
in a storm how to hide His jewels. God hid Jeremiah in
captivity. He hid a hundred prophets in a cave, 1 Kings
18:13. He hid several under His wings in the Marian
persecution. The Lord commanded His angel to seal
His servants on the forehead (a mark of safety) before
He opened His vial and poured His curses on the
earth, Revelation 9:4. It may be you shall be hid; nay, if
you discard your sins, you shall certainly be hid. You
shall be hid either above ground or below ground, Job
14:13. You shall be hid in the wounds of Christ, and
then you are safe. You shall escape, if not the stroke of
death, yet the sting of death. If your life is not spared,
yet your sin shall be pardoned. You shall be hid within
the veil. God will put all His elect jewels in the cabinet
of heaven.

USE 4. OF CONSOLATION

Here is a pillar of support to every soul who has broken off sin and espoused holiness. This is an undoubted evidence that you are a true child of God. Flesh and blood could not reach to this, only omnipotent grace could conquer your corruption. 1 John 3:9, "He who is born of God doth not commit sin." He does not sin deliberately. He does not sin with delight. In his heart, he abhors sin; in his life, he forsakes it. Here is one who is born of God. And let this comfort the real penitent. Though he cannot get rid of a body of sin, but may have his failings do what he can, yet these failings shall not be charged upon him, but his Surety. God will be propitious through Christ. He will take notice of the sincerity and pass by the infirmity.

3

An Alarm to Sinners

or
The Last and Great Change

"I will wait till my change come."
Job 14:14

If all that has been previously said will not stop men in their sins, I shall add little more; only let me make this one motion to them, that they would remember their mortality and think seriously how soon a change may come, and how terrible it will be to die in their sins, John 8:21. For this purpose, let them hearken to this deathwatch in the text, "I will wait till my change come."

This book of Job treats much of mortality. Job looked upon himself as a man who was not long for this world. Job 17:1, "The graves are ready for me." And he loved to be walking often among the tombs, and so to familiarize death to him. "I will wait till my change come."

"Till my change come"—that is, till death comes. So Aben Ezra, Drusius, and our Annotators render it.

In the text there is:

Job's resolution, "I will wait."

The length of time he will wait, "till my change come." From which words flow three propositions:

1. Death is a change.
2. This change will come.
3. It is a high part of Christian prudence to wait until this change comes.

DOCTRINE 1. Death is a change. There is a threefold change:

A change before death.
A change at death.
A change after death.

1. *There is a change before death.* Death being ready to approach changes a man's opinion. When a person comes to die, he has another opinion of things than he had before. He now sees with other eyes.

He now has another opinion of the world than he had. He sees what a vain thing it is. He could never see its nothingness, the devil having cast a mist before his eyes. He once doted upon the world. Now, all its jewels are pulled off and he sees it in its night dress. He sees how the world's paint falls off, and how unable it is to give one drop of true comfort at the hour of death.

Death approaching changes a man's opinion about sin. Before, he looked upon sin as merely a matter of merriment. He thought swearing an oath, drinking to excess, and wasting his precious time in vanity was but a light thing. He said of sin, as Lot did of Zoar, "Is it not a little one?" Genesis 19:20. But when he sees death's grim face appear, he now has other apprehensions of sin than he had before. The wine that showed its color in the glass and smiled at him now bites like a serpent, Proverbs 23:32. Those sins which before were thought to be light as feathers are now like talents of lead ready to sink him. King Belshazzar was carousing and drinking wine in the vessels of the Temple, but when there came forth "fingers of a man's hand, and wrote upon the wall, then the King's countenance was changed, and his thoughts troubled, so that the joints of his loins were loosed," Daniel 5:6. So, after sinful pleasure enjoyed, when death begins to show itself and put forth its fingers, and a man sees a dreadful hand-writing in his conscience, oh, how is his opinion about sin changed! How his thoughts trouble him! Now what would he give to have his sins pardoned? He never saw the face of sin as ugly as in the glass of death.

When death comes near a man, it changes his opinion about holiness. He once thought it a shame to be seen with a Bible in his hand. Holiness before was the object of his scorn and hatred. He called pious discourses "canting," repentance "whining," praying by the Spirit "babbling." He baptized true zeal with the name of frenzy. But when death begins to approach, it changes his judgment. He now sees how mistaken he was and that without holiness he can never see God, Hebrews 12:14. Now his eyes begin to be opened and he subscribes to that maxim, Job 28:28, "The fear of the Lord, that is wisdom." He now sees the best way to be safe is to be sincere. Oh, now what would he give for a dram of that holiness which before he despised! How glad he would be to die the death of the righteous, though he hated to live their life!

Thus, there is a change made not long before death. The sinner now sees himself in a snare and labyrinth. Now the minister must be sent for in all haste, though oftentimes he comes too late.

2. *There is a change at death.* This is a change in the body. Job 14:20, "Thou changest his countenance and sendest him away." The most ruddy complexion is strangely metamorphized when once the pale horse of death rides over it. The eyes are hollow. The cheeks are pale. The jaws are fallen. That beautiful face which once allured now frightens. Psalm 39:11, "Thou makest his beauty consume away like a moth." Death is a moth which consumes a beauty of the finest spinning. Hence, the body being so discolored by death and turned into an ill favor, the patriarchs desired to have their dead buried out of their sight, Genesis 23:4. Death so changes the body and puts it into such a frightful dress that none fall in love with it but the worms.

3. *There is a change after death.* This change is chiefly in regard to the soul. To the godly, it is a blessed change. To the wicked, it is a cursed change.

The godly, after death, have a blessed change. They have a full acquittal from their sins and are put into an actual possesion of their inheritance. Faith gives them a propriety in glory, and death gives them a possession. Oh, blessed change, from a desert to a paradise, from a house of mourning to a banquet house, from a bloody battle to a victorious crown! Glorified believers shall chance their place, but not their company, said Dr. (John) Preston. They shall have transforming sights of God. 1 John 3:2, "When He shall appear, we shall be like Him."

As the souls of the godly shall have a blessed change after death, so shall their bodies at the resurrection, John 6:40 and 1 Thessalonians 4:19. Though the grave is their long home, it is not their last home. Mother earth shall fall in travail and be delivered of the bodies of the saints, and they shall shine as the sun in its meridian splendor, Philippians 3:21.

Death will make a cursed change to the wicked. They must go out of the bed of pleasure, leave all their mirth and music. Revelation 18:21, "The voice of harpers and musicians shall be heard no more in thee." The wicked must change from joy to misery, from a temporary paradise to an eternal prison, Luke 16:19.

DOCTRINE 2. This change will come.

Death can no more be stopped in its race than the sun. Death's scythe cuts asunder the royal scepter. God's messenger of death finds out every man. Ecclesiastes 8:8, "There is no discharge in that war." Among men, if one is summoned to the wars he may find some excuse. He may plead unfitness or he may substitute another in his place. But in this war with death, the press is so strict that there is no getting off. "There is no discharge in that war." As death sends its challenge to all, so it is sure to conquer. When death, like God's sergeant-at-arms, arrests men, there is no bribing this sergeant or making resistance.

Death will not be bribed. It was a saying of a Mr. Beauford, a wicked bishop in King Henry the Sixth's time, "Wherefore should I die being so rich? Will not death be hired? Will money do nothing?" (Foxe's *Acts and Monuments*).

Ezekiel 7:19, "Their silver and gold shall not be able to deliver them in the day of the wrath of the Lord."

Death cannot be resisted. Take a man in his best estate. Let him be dignified with honor like Solomon, armed with strength like Sampson. Were his flesh as firm as the leviathan, yet the bullet of death would soon shoot through him. How easily can God look us into our grave! Men may set up their standards, but God always sets up the trophies.

That there must be a change is evident. The body, being but an earthly tabernacle, 2 Peter 1:14, the cords of it will soon be loosed. Besides, there is a decree of death passed upon all, Hebrews 9:27. And how soon this change will come we do not know. Death may be within a few days march of us, and when it comes with its letter of summons we must surrender.

USE 1. OF EXHORTATION

BRANCH 1. Let us all exercise ourselves to the thoughts of this great change. Let us not be of Otho the Emperor's mind, who judged it cowardly to think of death. Job 17:14, "I have said to corruption, Thou art my father, and to the worm, Thou art my mother." Job, by often meditating on death, was as well acquainted with it as with his father and mother. By often handling this serpent, it will be less frightful. The serious contemplation of this change would produce these four excellent effects.

FOUR EFFECTS OF CONTEMPLATING DEATH

1. It would humble us. Why should we set up the flags and banners of pride when we are but dust and

rottenness? The thoughts of the grave would bury our pride, Psalm 82:6.

2. The thoughts of a sudden change would be an antidote against sin. Shall we go on in sin when God may say this night, "Give an account of your stewardship"? The way to give sin a mortal wound is to set up a death's head, a cast of our face after we die.

In particular, the thoughts of our change would keep us from sinful compliance. Some Latitudinarians can cut their religion according to the fashion of the times. They can be Protestant or Papist. They can sail with any wind that blows preferment. But that man will not be for every change who thinks seriously of his last change.

3. The thoughts of this change would cure our inordinate love of the world. A change will come shortly, and then what will this world be to us? All our money will serve only to buy us a burial sheet. Saladine, the Turk, lying at the point of death, commanded that a white sheet should be carried before him to his grave on the point of a spear with this proclamation, "These are the rich spoils which Saladine the Emperor carries away with him, of all his triumphs and victories obtained, of all his realms possessed, nothing is left him but this sheet." After a great feast comes the basket for leftover food. Shortly, death, like such a basket, will take away all our earthly comforts.

4. The serious thoughts of our last and great change would make us spend our time better. How diligent men would be in reading, how fervent in prayer, how watchful over our hearts, how useful in our relations! We would live every day as if it were our dying day. He who knows how short his time is in his

farm will make the best advantage of it. He who re-
members the shortness of his time here, and how soon
a change may come, will improve all the seasons of
grace for his soul that he may give a good account of
his stewardship. The nearer things are to the center,
the swifter is their motion.

BRANCH 2. Let us prepare for this change. All the
changes we meet with in the world are but to fit us for
our last change. Men unprepared, being summoned by
the king of terror before God's tribunal, go as the
prisoner to the bar to receive their fatal doom. I think
the thoughts of it are enough to put them either into
frenzy or despair. Would it not be sad for a man to
have his house on fire, and the fire so fierce that he
has no time to get out his goods? Such is the case of
many at death. A fever has set their house of clay on
fire, and they are snatched away so suddenly that they
have no time to make provision for their souls.

QUESTION. What shall we do to be fitted for our
last change?

ANSWER 1. Let us labor to get into Christ. It is terrible when death finds any out of Christ. As if the
avenger of blood had overtaken the manslayer before
he had gotten to the city of refuge. You who are in
Christ are as the dove in the rock. Romans 8:1, "There
is no condemnation to them which are in Christ Jesus."
Christ has fully satisfied for believers. Christ's blood
turns a deathbed into a bed of roses.

The best way to be fitted for dying is being married
to Christ. No matter if death unties the knot between
the body and the soul as long as faith has tied the knot
between Christ and the soul. The Prince of Peace se-

cures against the king of terror.

ANSWER 2. If we would be fitted for our last change, let us labor for a spiritual change. Before our bodies are changed, let us labor to have our hearts changed. O let us get the holy anointing, 1 John 2:27. Grace is as needful for the soul as oil is for the lamp and as breath for the body. John 3:7, "Ye must be born again." He who is born but once shall die twice. Grace makes an admirable change. To be changed from sin to holiness is as if iron were changed into gold or dust into a pearl. Now, the soul is all glorious within. O labor for this gracious change! At death, a good face may change for the worse, but a good heart changes for the better.

DOCTRINE 3. It is a high point of Christian prudence to wait till our changes comes. "I will wait."

Waiting implies two things:

Expectation. "I will wait for my change"—that is, I will look for it. A gracious soul is ever expecting to hear new of his going home. Death does not come to a child of God unawares, but it come as Jonathan's arrow did to David, who went into the field and expected where the arrow should be shot, 1 Samuel 20:24. A godly man looks every hour for the arrow of death to be shot at him.

Diligence. "I will wait till my change come"—that is, I will be setting my soul in order for death. We must not wait and sit still, but wait and work. He who waits for his master's coming will be careful that everything is in good decorum. Matthew 24:26, "Blessed is that servant whom his Lord when he cometh, shall find so doing." Be often calling yourselves to account; every night review what you have been doing all the day. This is the right waiting for our change, when we put our souls in a ready posture for death and judgment.

USE 2. OF REPROOF

BRANCH 1. It reproves such as are so far from waiting for their change that they cannot endure to think of their change. They are no more willing to think of death than a man drowned in debt is to think of going to prison. Amos 6:3, "Ye that put far away the evil day." Men are generally set upon pleasure. If they go to hell, they would go there merrily. Who even thinks of his change? He hopes for long life. The bud of youth hopes to come to the flower of age, and the flower of age hopes to come to old age, and old age hopes to renew its strength as the eagle. Psalm 49:11, "Their inward thought is that their houses shall continue forever." That would rather be blazing their shield than providing their tombstone. The lustful flirt does not like the noise of a passing bell, and the powdered hair forgets the dust.

BRANCH 2. It reproves such as wait, but not in the right sense. They wait to fulfill their lusts. "They eye of the adulterer waits for the twilight," Job 24:15. The unjust man waits for an opportunity to defraud. Is this to wait as Job did? Where do men wait for their change? In a tavern, at a theater, in a whorehouse? Alas, their change comes before they are aware. The graves are ready for them, but they are not ready for their graves.

USE 3. OF EXHORTATION

It exhorts Christians to wait for their change. As the husbandman waits till his seed sown springs up, as the merchant waits for the coming home of his ship, so we should wait till death comes to ship us over to another world.

1. Let us wait with watchfulness. Mark 13:33, "Watch and pray." Let us watch our hearts that they neither decoy us into sin nor charm us asleep in security.

2. Let us wait with patience. "I will wait till my change come." The Septuagint renders it, "I will be patient."

The sufferings the godly endure in this life, and the joys they hope for after death, may put them upon desiring a change. But though they should covet to die, yet they must be content to live. Wait with patience till the appointed time has come. The Father knows when the best season is to send his child home. Christian, do not be desirous to be in heaven before your time. Wait but awhile and you shall have what you have prayed and wept for. 'Tis but awhile and God will take the cross off your shoulders and set a crown upon your head.

4

The Furnace Heated Hotter

or
A Clear Description of Such Persons as shall have a Greater Share in Hell Torments.

"These shall receive greater damnation."
Mark 12:40

I had thought to have stopped my pen here, but supposing the largest discourses of this nature are little enough to divert wicked persons from their excesses, I have one word more to add, that if sinners have not lost their reason, they would be persuaded to reflect a little and consider seriously the damnableness of their state after this life, and lay to heart this text dropped from our Savior's own lips, "These shall receive greater damnation."

I do not intend to meddle with the context, but shall take the words as they lie entirely in themselves. In the text there are three parts:

A fiery furnace: damnation.

The furnace heated hotter: greater damnation.

The persons for whom this furnace is doubly

heated: "These shall receive."

DOCTRINE. The proposition I intend is this: There are some sorts of sinners who shall be more severely tormented in hell than others. "These shall receive greater damnation."

In respect of the duration of torment, so all shall be punished alike. All the black regiment of reprobates shall lie in hell forever. But in respect of the degree of torment, all shall not be punished alike. Some shall have a more fiery indignation than others, Hebrews 10:27. They who have the least punishment in hell shall have enough. The coolest part of hell is hot enough, but there are some who shall have a hotter place in hell than others. All shall go into that fiery prison, but some sinners God will thrust into the dungeon. Those whose impieties are more fearfully accented and who have sinned at a higher rate than others, God will take His full blow at in hell and will tear them in His wrath, Psalm 50:22. For such, He will heat the infernal furnace seven times hotter. I shall briefly give you a list and catalogue of such sinners as dying in impenitence shall receive greater damnation.

SINNERS WHO SHALL RECEIVE GREATER DAMNATION

1. *Such as are willfully ignorant.* It is one thing not to know and another to be unwilling to know. They might have the notion of the true God, but they will not. They trample upon this pearl of divine knowledge. They not only neglect knowledge but reject it. Hosea

4:6, "Because thou hast rejected knowledge." Or, as the
Hebrew word signifies, "thou hast hated it." The Ethio-
pians curse the sun, so did they the light of saving
knowledge. These knowledge despisers shall have a
greater share in the torments of hell. Isaiah 27:11, "It is
a people of no understanding, therefore He that made
them will have no mercy on them, and He that formed
them will show them no favor." And for God to show
no favor is to take the extremity of the Law upon them.

2. *Such as will neither follow the thing that is good for
themselves, nor yet allow others.* Luke 11:52, "Ye entered
not in yourselves, and them that were entering in ye
hindered." Such as will neither read the Bible themselves nor endure that their children should; such as
will neither hear a good sermon themselves nor endure that their neighbors should; such as will stop the
pipes which are to convey the water of life and who
eclipse the lamps of the sanctuary—these shall receive
greater damnation. 1 Thessalonians 2:16, "Forbidding
us to speak to the Gentiles that they might be saved, to
fill up their sins alway, for the wrath is come upon
them to the uttermost."

3. *Such as sin against clear illuminations and convictions.*
These the Apostle speaks of, James 4:17, "Who know to
do good but do it not." They are not ignorant that the
things they do are sin. Conscience, like the cherubims,
stands with a flaming sword to deter them, yet they will
eat the apple of pleasure though they die. These men's
sins have an emphasis. They sin with a witness. This
made the sin of the fallen angels so great, for which
they lie in chains. They had no ignorance, no passion

to stir them up, no temptation, but they sinned volun-
tarily and out of pure choice. This sinning against conscience is accompanied:

With pride. Sinners know the mind of God, yet act
contrarily to it. They set their will above God's will.
They say in their heart as did Pharaoh, Exodus 5:2,
"Who is the Lord that I should obey His voice?"

With impudence. Let what will come on it, let God
take it well or ill, men will pursue their sins. Here the
veil of modest is laid aside.

If God has been so terrible against sins of infirmity
and passion, as we see in Moses and Uzzah, how fierce
will His anger be against pertinacious offenders!

Sins against illumination and conviction make deep
wounds in the soul. Other sins fetch blood; these are a
stab in the heart. Every little hole in the roof lets in
rain, but a crack in the foundation endangers the fall
of the house. Every sin of weakness is prejudicial, but
sins against illumination crack the conscience and
threaten the ruin of the soul. To sin in this matter
makes sin the heavier and hell the hotter.

Consider this, all you who rebel against gospel light.
If you do not repent, you will be more scorched in hell.
Luke 12:47, "That servant which knew his Lord's will,
and did not according to his will, shall doubtless be
beaten with many stripes."

4. *Such as are plotters and contrivers of sin.* Psalm 36:4,
He deviseth mischief upon his head." Many men's
heads ache till they have found out some new mischief.
Such were those presidents who invented a decree
against Daniel and got the king to sign it, Daniel 6:9.
These inventers of evil things shall be more plagued in

hell than others. He who first plots a treason is counted the capital offender and has the most exquisite tortures. Micah 2:1, "Woe to them that devise iniquity." This woe is as a talent of lead to sink them deeper into damnation.

5. *Such as are haters of holiness.* The diamond of grace is hated because of its sparkling luster. If men hate the saints for their grace, how they would hate Christ if He were now upon the earth! Will God lay those in His bosom who hate Him? No, they shall have a lower place in hell than others. Deuteronomy 7:10, "And repayeth them that hate Him to their face, He will not be slack to him that hateth Him, He will repay him to his face." The repetition shows both the verity and severity of their punishment.

6. *Such as are lovers of sin.* Jerome said that it is worse to love sin than to commit it. He who loves sin, his heart is in the sin. He follows it like a man does his game with delight, Jeremiah 11:15. Sinners say they hate the devil, but they love that which will bring them to the devil. Lovers of sin shall have more of hell torment. The fire will make them forget the pleasure. Revelation 22:15, "Without are dogs, and whatsoever loveth and maketh a lie." It is bad enough to tell a lie, but he who loves a lie shall lie lower in hell.

7. *They shall have a greater degree of torment who persecute the saints of the Most High.* Acts 7:52, "Which of the prophets have not your fathers persecuted?" The godly are called sheep and the wicked called briars. These briars tear not only the wool, but the flesh of the

sheep. These shall be more fearfully punished. What they are to endure afterwards may be witnessed by the hell many of them feel in their conscience and by the judgments of God upon them in this life.

Charles IX of France, who shed so much Protestant blood in the massacre at Paris that it dyed the rivers a crimson color, was struck by God with an excessive bleeding in several parts of his body, to the amazement of the beholders. If God in this life ordains His arrows against the persecutors, Psalm 7:13, then surely He will make them His standing mark in hell, at which He will be shooting to all eternity.

8. *Such as are seemingly good so that they may be really bad, who make profession a specious presence for their wickedness so that, under this mask, they may lie and deceive.* They do the devil's work in Christ's uniform. Proverbs 7:14, "This day have I paid my vows, come let us take our fill of love." Who would have suspected this harlot, having been at church? She made her devotion a preface to adultery. Luke 20:47, "Which devour widow's houses, and for a show make long prayers, the same shall receive greater damnation." To make long prayers for this end, that they might do unrighteous actions, was damnable hypocrisy. If there is anyone who makes religion a political engine to carry on their sin more smoothly, these shall lie in the hottest place of hell.

9. *Such as do no works of mercy.* They are akin to the Church. Nabal said, 1 Samuel 25:11, "Shall I take my bread and water, and give it unto men whom I knew not?" Their hearts are hardened against Christ's poor. Their money cannot be called "quick silver." It does

not come so quickly from them. These shall have a greater portion in hell torments. James 2:13, "He shall have judgment without mercy, that hath showed no mercy." He shall have torment and nothing but torment. A person may as well be cruel by not relieving the poor as by wronging him. And such a one shall have judgment without mercy.

10. *Such as die under final unbelief.* Many think none are to be counted infidels but Turks and pagans. Yes, there are many infidel Christians. They do not believe God's veracity and holiness. They do not have as much faith as devils, James 2:19. Infidelity is linked with impenitence. Acts 19:9, "Divers were hardened and believed not." Unbelief gives God the lie, 1 John 5:10. Therefore, such persons are put in the forefront of those who go to hell. Revelation 21:8, "The unbelieving shall have a part in the lake which burneth with fire."

11. *Such as have grown gray under the gospel but are never the better.* Divers have enjoyed the prayers, tears, and studies of God's choicest ministers. They have been put in the fattest pastures of ordinances, but yet they may say with the Prophet, "My leanness, my leanness," Isaiah 24:16. They have had warm preaching but they freeze in the sun. They can hear ministers preach the most startling doctrine and see them throw the flashes of hellfire about in the congregation, but their consciences are no more stirred than the pillars in the church. Proud they were and they are proud still. Profane they were and they are profane still. All the sermons they have heard are like the showers falling

on a rock which is never made softer or more fruitful.
"The bellows are burnt, the lead consumed," Jeremiah
6:29. The lungs of ministers are spent, but no refining
work of grace has passed upon them. These certainly
shall have greater degrees of torment.

If heathens who never heard of Christ are damned,
these shall be double-damned. Matthew 11:23, "Thou
Capernaum who art exalted unto heaven shalt be
brought down to hell, for if the mighty works which
have been done in thee had been done in Sodom, it
would have remained until this day, but I say unto you,
that it shall be more tolerable for the land of Sodom in
the day of judgment than for thee." In Capernaum
were the oracles of God. There Jesus Christ preached,
there He worked miracles. Therefore, by not repenting
and believing, she was in a worse condition than
Sodom and should be more severely punished.

You who have had God's golden candlestick among
you and are not more holy, it would have been better
to have lived in America where Christ had never been
preached than in Europe or London. It will be better
with Indians than such Christians as live in the bosom
of the unreformed Church.

12. *Such as die with the falling sickness, who apostatize
and fall away from the truth.* There are some in this age
who have not only lost their former strictness in religion, but the very leaves of their profession are
dropped off. As their sin is more odious because their
apostasy brings a scandal upon the ways of God, so
their punishment shall be answerable. These rene-
gades shall be hung up in chains in hell. Hebrews
10:38, "If any man draw back (or, as it is in the Greek,

if he steals as a soldier from his colors) My soul shall have no pleasure in him." It is as if God should say, "I will execute the fierceness of My anger upon him. He shall drink the dregs of the cup of wrath, and that cup shall never pass away from him."

13. *Such Ishmael spirits as scoff at religion.* The Apostle has foretold it as a sin of the last times. 2 Peter 3:3, "There shall come in the last days scoffers." This is fearful, when men have arrived at such a height of impiety as, with Lucian, to deride holy walking. The tongue of the scoffers is the devil's gun out of which he shoots his bullets against religion. There are some who, though they are not good themselves, yet they have a venerable esteem of those who are good. Herod reverenced John the Baptist. But such the devil has taken great possession of who reproach others for that wherein they most resemble God. Take heed of this sin, said Latimer, for I never knew but one scorner who repented. Scoffers are, for the most part, atheists. When men have outfaced their conscience and lost all principle of ingenuity and modesty, then they fall a-scoffing. These shall have greater damnation. Isaiah 28:22, "Be no mockers, lest your bands be made strong." You shall be bound in chains of darkness, and these bands shall be made strong.

14. *Such as have perverted others by their corrupt writings.* They have set forth books full of error, and others have sucked in the poison of those books and been damned. Some have published to the world that moral virtue does not differ from grace, and so have caused people to rest in their moralities, never aspiring after the New

Birth. Alas, a man may keep a civil decorum, yet there may be some sin that reigns in his heart. The Pharisee could say, "I am no adulterer," Luke 18:11, but he could not say, "I am not proud." Civility may curb but it cannot change.

The Socinians have broached many damnable errors in print against the deity of Christ. These shall drink deeper in the cup of wrath. Matthew 5:19, "Whosoever shall break one of these commandments, and shall teach men so, he shall be called the least in the Kingdom of Heaven." That is, he shall never come there. If the breakers of God's law are punished seven-fold, then those who teach men to break them shall be punished seventy and seven-fold. Revelation 19:20, "The false prophet was taken (he who by his errors had deceived the world) and was cast alive into the midst of the lake of fire."

15. *Such as make their bodies* (which should be the temples of the Holy Ghost) *vessels of uncleanness.* Those who burn in lust shall one day (without repentance) burn in hotter flames than others, 2 Peter 2:9. O who would, for a cup of pleasure, drink a sea of wrath?

16. *Such as send other men to hell by their bad example.* The drunken master has made his servant to reel by his example. The swearing father has taught his son to swear and damned him by his example. Would it not be something to be lamented if the child should get the plague of his father and die? And is it not often so, in a spiritual sense, that the father poisons and infects his child by his cursed example? Doubtless, such monsters in wickedness shall have a greater portion in hell

torments. They shall not only be damned for their own sins but for other men's sins. This was the reason why Dives desired that some might go preach to his brethren, that they might not come to hell. He had given his brethren a bad example, and he thought that if they were sentenced to hell his torments would be increased and he would be punished for their sins as well as his own.

USE. OF EXHORTATION

BRANCH 1. As we should take heed of living in any sin (for the least sin lived in and unrepented of will bring us to hell), so especially let us take heed of being in the black bedroll of these sinners I have now mentioned. These dying in final impenitence shall be more severely punished. A greater millstone of wrath will fall upon their head. If a spark or two of God's anger is so grievous, what is it when He shall stir up all His wrath, Psalm 78:38?

BRANCH 2. Let us labor to fly to Christ by faith. Let us get Him to stand like a screen between us and the fire of God's indignation. Romans 8:1, "There is no condemnation to them that are in Christ Jesus." God the Father will not condemn them because He is satisfied in the price paid for them. He will not require the debt twice, from both the Surety and the debtor. And Jesus Christ will not condemn them, for believers are His spouse; and Christ will not condemn His own spouse. So that, if ever we would be safe, let us get into Christ, and being in this city of refuge, God's justice, that avenger of blood, will not touch us. Having put on the garment of our Lord's righteousness, the fire of hell can never singe this garment. 1 Thessalonians 1:10, "Jesus hath delivered us from the wrath to come."

Appendix

The Mystery of the Lord's Supper

"And as they were eating, Jesus took bread, and blessed it, and brake it, and gave it to the disciples, and said, Take, eat; this is My body. And He took the cup, and gave thanks, and gave it to them saying, Drink ye all of it; for this is My blood of the New Testament, which is shed for many for the remission of sins." Matthew 26:26-28

In these words, we have the institution of the Lord's Supper. The Greeks call the sacrament "a mystery." There is in it a mystery of wonder and a mystery of mercy. "The celebration of the Lord's Supper," said Chrysostom, "is the commemoration of the greatest blessing that ever the world enjoyed." A sacrament is a visible sermon. And herein the sacrament excels the Word preached. The Word is a trumpet to proclaim Christ. The sacrament is a glass to represent Him.

QUESTION. But why was the Sacrament of the Lord's Supper appointed? Is not the Word sufficient to bring us to heaven?

ANSWER. The Word is for the engrafting; the

Sacraments are for the confirming of faith. The
Word brings us to Christ; the Sacrament builds us
up in Him. The Word is the font where we are baptized with the Holy Ghost; the Sacrament is the table
where we are fed and cherished. The Lord conde-
scends to our weakness. Were we made up all of
spirit, there would be no need of bread and wine.
But we are compounded creatures. Therefore God,
to help our faith, not only gives us an audible word
but a visible sign. I may here allude to that saying of
our Savior, "Except ye see signs, ye will not believe,"
John 4:48. Christ sets His body and blood before us
in the elements. Here are signs, else we will not believe.

Things taken in by the eye work more upon us
than things taken in by the ear. A solemn spectacle
of mortality more affects us than an oration. So,
when we see Christ broken in the bread and, as it
were, crucified before us, this more affects our
hearts than the bare preaching of the Word.

So I come to the text. "As they were eating, Jesus
took bread." Where I shall open these five particu-
lars in reference to the Sacrament:

1. The Author.
2. The Time.
3. The Manner.
4. The Guests.
5. The Benefits.

1. The Author of the Sacrament, Jesus Christ.
"Jesus took bread." To institute sacraments belongs,
by right, to Christ, and is a flower of His crown. He
only who can give grace can appoint the sacra-

ments, which are the seals of grace. Christ, being the Founder of the Sacrament, gives a glory and luster to it. A king making a feast adds more state and magnificence to it. "Jesus took bread," He whose name is above every name, God blessed forever, Philippians 2:9.

2. The time when Christ instituted the Sacrament; wherein we may take notice of two circumstances:

1. *It was when He had supped;* "after supper," Luke 22:20, which had this mystery in it, to show that the Sacrament is chiefly intended as a spiritual banquet. It was not to indulge the senses, but to feast the graces. It was "after supper."

2. *The other circumstance of time is that Christ appointed the Sacrament a little before His sufferings.* "The Lord Jesus, the same night in which He was betrayed, took bread," 1 Corinthians 11:23. He knew troubles were now coming upon His disciples. It would be no small perplexity to them to see their Lord and Master crucified. And shortly after they must pledge Him in a bitter cup. Therefore, to arm them against such a time and to animate their spirits, that very night in which He was betrayed He gives them His body and blood in the Sacrament.

This may give us a good hint that, in all trouble of mind, especially approaches of danger, it is needful to have recourse to the Lord's Supper. The Sacrament is both an antidote against fear and a restorative to faith. The night in which Christ was betrayed, He took bread.

3. The manner of the institution; wherein four

things are observable: (1) The taking of the bread;
(2) The breaking of it; (3) The blessing of it; and (4)
The administering of the cup.

1. *The taking of the bread.* "Jesus took bread."

QUESTION. What is meant by this phrase, "He
took bread?"

ANSWER. Christ's taking and separating the
bread from common uses holds forth a double mystery.

First, it signified that God in His eternal decree
set Christ apart for the work of our redemption. He
was separate from sinners, Hebrews 7:26.

Second, Christ's setting the elements apart from
common bread and wine showed that He is not for
common persons to feed upon. They are to be di-
vinely purified who touch these holy things of God.
They must be outwardly separated from the world
and inwardly sanctified by the Spirit.

QUESTION. Why did Christ take bread rather
than any other element?

ANSWER 1. Because it prefigured Him. Christ
was typified by the show-bread, 1 Kings 7:48; by the
bread which Melchisedek offered unto Abraham,
Genesis 14:18; and by the cake which the angel
brought to Elijah, 1 Kings 19:6. Therefore, He took
bread to answer the type.

ANSWER 2. Christ took bread because of the
analogy. Bread resembled Him closely. "I am that
Bread of life," John 6:48. There is a three-fold resem-
blance:

Bread is useful. Other comforts are more for delight than use. Music delights the ear, colors the
eye, but bread is the staff of life. So Christ is useful.

There is no subsisting without Him. "He that eateth Me, even he shall live by Me," John 6:57.

Bread is satisfying. If a man is hungry, flowers or pictures do not satisfy, but bread does. So Jesus Christ, the Bread of the soul, satisfies. He satisfies the eye with beauty, the heart with sweetness, the conscience with peace.

Bread is strengthening. "Bread which strengthens man's heart," Psalm 104:15. So Christ, the Bread of the soul, transmits strength. He strengthens us against temptations and for doing and suffering work. He is like the cake the angel brought to the prophet. "He arose and did eat, and went in the strength of that meat forty days and forty nights, unto Horeb the mount of God," 1 Kings 19:8.

2. *The second thing in the institution is the breaking of the bread.* "He brake it." This shadowed out Christ's death and passion with all the torments of His body and soul. "It pleased the Lord to bruise Him," Isaiah 53:10. When the spices are bruised, then they send forth a sweet savor. So, when Christ was bruised on the cross, He sent out a fragrant smell. Christ's body crucifying was the breaking open of a box of precious ointment which filled heaven and earth with its perfume.

QUESTION. But why was Christ's body broken? What was the cause of His suffering?

ANSWER. Surely not for any desert of His own. "The Messiah shall be cut off, but not for Himself," Daniel 9:26. In the original it is, "He shall be cut off, and there is nothing in Him." There is no cause in Him why He should suffer. When the high priest

went into the tabernacle, offered first "for himself,"
Hebrews 9:7. Though he had his mitre or golden
plate, and wore holy garments, yet he was not pure
and innocent. He must offer sacrifice for himself as
well as the people. But Jesus Christ, that great High
Priest, though He offered a bloody sacrifice, yet it
was not for Himself.

Why, then, was His blessed body broken? It was
for our sins. "He was wounded for our transgressions," Isaiah 53:5. The Hebrew word for "wounded"
has a double emphasis. Either it may signify that He
was pierced through as with a dart, or that He was
profaned. He was used as some common vile thing,
and Christ can thank us for it. "He was wounded for
our transgressions." So that, if the question were put
to us, as once was put to Christ, "Prophesy, who
smote Thee?" Luke 22:64, we might soon answer that
it was our sins that smote Him. Our pride made
Christ wear a crown of thorns. As Zipporah said to
Moses, "A bloody husband art thou to me," Exodus
4:25, so may Christ say to His church, "A bloody
spouse you have been to Me; you have cost Me My
heart's blood."

QUESTION. But how could Christ suffer, being
God? The Godhead is impassible.

ANSWER. Christ suffered only in the human nature, not the Divine. Damascen expresses it by this
simile: If one pours water on iron that is red hot, the
fire suffers by the water and is extinguished; but the
iron does not suffer. So the human nature of Christ
might suffer death, but the Divine nature is not ca-
pable of any passion. When Christ was in the human

nature, He was in the Divine nature triumphing. As we wonder at the rising of the Son of righteousness in His incarnation, so we may wonder at the going down of this Sun in His passion.

QUESTION. But if Christ suffered only in His human nature, how could His suffering satisfy for sin?

ANSWER. By reason of the hypostatic union, the human nature being united to the Divine. The human nature suffered; the Divine nature satisfied. Christ's Godhead gave both majesty and efficacy to His sufferings. Christ was Sacrifice, Priest, and Altar. He was Sacrifice, as He was man; Priest, as He was God and man; Altar, as He was God. It is the property of the altar to sanctify the thing offered on it, Matthew 23:19. So the altar of Christ's Divine nature sanctified the sacrifice of His death and made it meritorious.

Now, concerning Christ's suffering upon the cross, observe these things:

The bitterness of it to Him. "He was broken." The very thoughts of His suffering put Him into an agony. "Being in agony, He prayed more earnestly, and He sweat, as it were, great drops of blood falling down to the ground," Luke 22:44. He was full of sorrow. "My soul is exceeding sorrowful, even unto death," Matthew 26:38.

Christ's crucifixion was:

1. A lingering death. It was more for Christ to suffer one hour than for us to have suffered forever. But His death was lengthened out. He hung three hours on the cross. He died many deaths before He

could die one.

2. It was a painful death. His hands and feet were nailed, which parts, being full of sinews, and therefore very tender, His pain must be most acute and sharp. And to have the envenomed arrow of God's wrath shot to His heart, this was the direful catastrophe, and caused that outcry upon the cross, "My God, My God, why hast Thou forsaken Me?" The justice of God was now enflamed and heightened to its full. "God spared not His Son," Romans 8:38. Nothing must be abated of the debt. Christ felt the pains of hell, though not locally, yet equivalently. In the Sacrament, we see this tragedy acted before us.

3. It was a shameful death. Christ was hung between two thieves, Matthew 27:38. It was as if He had been the principal malefactor. Well might the lamp of heaven withdraw its light and mask itself with darkness, as blushing to behold the Sun of righteousness in an eclipse. It is hard to say which was greater, the blood of the cross or the shame of the cross, Hebrews 12:2.

4. It was a cursed death, Deuteronomy 21:23. This kind of death was deemed exceedingly execrable, yet the Lord Jesus underwent this, "Being made a curse for us," Galatians 3:13. He who was God blessed forever, Romans 9:5, was under a curse.

Also, consider the sweetness of it to us. Christ's bruising is our healing. "By His stripes, we are healed," Isaiah 53:5. Calvin calls the crucifixion of Christ the hinge on which our salvation turns. Luther calls it a gospel spring opened to refresh sinners. Indeed, the suffering of Christ is a deathbed cordial. It is an antidote to expel all our fear.

Does sin trouble? Christ has overcome it for us. Besides the two thieves crucified with Christ, there were two other invisible thieves crucified with Him: sin and the devil.

3. *The third thing in the institution is Christ's blessing of the bread.* "He blessed it." This was the consecration of the elements. Christ, by His blessing, sanctified them and made them symbols of His body and blood. Christ's consecrating of the elements points out three things:

Christ, in blessing the elements, opened the nature of the Sacrament to the apostles. He explained this mystery. Christ advertised them, that as surely as they received the elements corporeally, so surely they received Him into their hearts spiritually.

Christ's blessing the elements signified His prayer for a blessing upon the ordinance. He prayed that these symbols of bread and wine might, through the blessing and operation of the Holy Ghost, sanctify the elect and seal up all spiritual mercies and privileges to them.

Christ's blessing the elements was His giving thanks. So it is in the Greek, "He gave thanks." Christ gave thanks that God the Father had, in the infinite riches of His grace, given His Son to expiate the sins of the world. And if Christ gave thanks, how may we give thanks! If He gave thanks who was to shed His blood, how may we give thanks who are to drink it! Christ also gave thanks that God had given these elements of bread and wine to not only be signs but seals of our redemption. As the seal serves to make over a conveyance of land, so the Sacra-

ment, as a spiritual seal, serves to make over Christ
and heaven to such as worthily receive it.

4. *The fourth particular in the institution is Christ's administering the cup.* "And He took the cup." The taking
of the cup showed the redundancy of merit in Christ
and the copiousness of our redemption. Christ was
not sparing. He not only gave us the bread but the
cup. We may say as the psalmist, "With the Lord is
plenteous redemption," Psalm 130:7.

If Christ gave the cup, how dare the papists with-
hold it? They clip and mutilate the ordinance. They
plot out Scripture and may fear that doom, "If any
man shall take away from the words of the book of
this prophecy, God shall take away his part out of
the book of life," Revelation 22:19.

QUESTION. What is meant by Christ's taking
the cup?

ANSWER. The cup is figurative; it is a metonymy
of the subject. The cup is put for the wine in it. By
this, Christ signified the shedding of His blood
upon the cross. When His blood was poured out,
now the vine was cut and bled. Now was the lily of
the valleys dyed a purple color. This was, to Christ, a
cup of astonishment, Ezekiel 23:33. But to us, it is a
cup of salvation. When Christ drank this cup of
blood, we may truly say that He drank a toast to the
world. It was precious blood, 1 Peter 1:19. In this
blood, we see sin fully punished and fully pardoned.
Well may the spouse give Christ of her spiced wine
and the juice of her pomegranate, Song of Solomon
8:2, when Christ has given her a draft of His warm
blood, spiced with His love and perfumed with the

Divine nature.

4. The fourth thing is the guests invited to this supper, or the persons to whom Christ distributed the elements. "He gave to His disciples and said, Take, eat." The Sacrament is children's bread. If a man makes a feast, he calls his friends. Christ calls His disciples; if He had any piece better than another, He carves it to them.

"This is My body which is given for you," Luke 22:19, that is, for you believers. Christ gave His body and blood to the disciples chiefly under this notion, that they were believers. As Christ poured out His prayers, John 17:9, so His blood only for believers. See how near to Christ's heart all believers lie! Christ's body was broken on the cross and His blood shed for them. The election has obtained it, Romans 11:7. Christ has passed by others, and died intentionally for them. Impenitent sinners have no benefit by Christ's death unless it is a short reprieve. Christ is given to the wicked in wrath. He is a Rock of offence, 1 Peter 2:8. Christ's blood is like chemical drops of oil which recover some patients, but kill others. Judas sucked death from the tree of life. God can turn stones into bread, and a sinner can turn bread into stones—the bread of life into the stone of stumbling.

5. The fifth thing observable in the text is the benefit of this supper in these words, "for the remission of sins." This is a mercy of the first magnitude, the crowning blessing. "Who forgiveth thy iniquities, who crowneth thee with loving-kindness,"

Psalm 103:3-4. Whosoever has this charter granted is enrolled in the book of life. "Blessed is he whose transgression is forgiven," Psalm 32:1. Under this word, "remission of sin," by a synecdoche, are comprehended all heavenly benedictions, justification, adoption, and glory—in respect of which benefits we may, with Chrysostom, call the Lord's Supper "the feast of the cross."

USE 1. This doctrine of the Sacrament confutes the opinion of transubstantiation. When Christ said, "This is My body," the papists affirm that the bread, after the consecration, is turned into the substance of Christ's body. We hold that Christ's body is in the Sacrament spiritually. But the papists say that it is there carnally, which opinion is both absurd and impious.

Absurd. For it is contrary, first, to Scripture. The Scripture asserts that Christ's body is locally and numerically in heaven. "Whom the heavens must receive until the times of restitution of all things," Acts 3:21. If Christ's body is circumscribed in heaven, then it cannot be materially in the eucharist. Second, it is contrary to reason. How is it imaginable that a thing should be changed into another species, yet continue the same? that the bread in the Sacrament should be transmuted and turned into flesh, yet remain bread still? When Moses' rod was turned into a serpent, it could not be at the same time both a rod and a serpent. That the bread in the Sacrament should be changed into the body of Christ, and yet remain bread, is a perfect contradiction. If the papist says that the bread is vanished, this is more fit to be put into their legend than our creed, for the color, form, and relish of the bread still remains.

Impious. This opinion of transubstantiation is impious, as appears in two things. First, it is a profaning of Christ's body. For if the bread in the Sacrament is the real body of Christ, then it may be eaten not only by the wicked but by reptiles and vermin, which were to disparage and cast contempt upon Christ and His ordinance. Second, it runs men inevitably upon sin. For through this mistake, that the bread is Christ's very body, there follows the Divine worship given to the bread—which is idolatry—as also the offering up of the bread, or host, in the mass, which is a blasphemy against Christ's priestly office, Hebrews 10:14, as if His sacrifice on the cross were imperfect.

Therefore, I conclude with Peter Martyr that this doctrine of transubstantiation is to be abhorred and exploded, being minted only in men's fancies but not sprung up in the field of the Holy Scriptures.

Also, this doctrine of the Sacrament confutes such as look upon the Lord's Supper only as an empty figure or shadow, resembling Christ's death, but having no intrinsic efficacy in it. Surely, this glorious ordinance is more than an effigy or representative of Christ. Why is the Lord's Supper called the communion of the body of Christ, 1 Corinthians 10:16, but because, in the right celebration of it, we have sweet communion with Christ? In this gospel ordinance, Christ not only shows forth His beauty, but sends forth His virtue. The Sacrament is not only a picture drawn, but a breast drawn. It gives us a taste of Christ as well as a sight, 1 Peter 2:3. Such as make the Sacrament only a representative of Christ shoot short of the mystery and come short of the comfort.

USE 2. It informs us of several things.

1. *It shows us the necessity of coming to the Lord's Supper.* Has Jesus Christ been at all this cost to make a feast? Then, surely, there must be guests, Luke 22:19. It is not left to our choice whether we will come or not; it is a duty purely indispensable. "Let him eat of that bread," 1 Corinthians 11:28, which words are not only permissive, but authoritative. It is as if a king should say, "Let it be enacted."

The neglect of the Sacrament runs men into a gospel penalty. It was infinite goodness in Christ to broach that blessed vessel of His body and let His sacred blood stream out. It is evil for us wilfully to omit such an ordinance wherein the trophy of mercy is so richly displayed and our salvation so nearly concerned. Well may Christ take this as an undervaluing of Him, and interpret it as no better than a bidding Him to keep His feast to Himself. He who did not observe the passover was to be cut off, Numbers 9:13. How angry was Christ with those who stayed away from the supper! They thought to put it off with a compliment. But Christ knew how to construe their excuse for a refusal. "None of those men which were bidden shall taste of My supper," Luke 14:24. Rejecting gospel mercy is a sin of so deep a die that God can do no less than punish it for a contempt. Some need a flaming sword to keep them from the Lord's Table, and others need Christ's whip of small cords to drive them to it.

Perhaps, some will say, they are above the Sacrament. It would be strange to hear a man say that he is above his food! The apostles were not above this ordinance, and does anyone presume to be a peg higher than the apostles? Let all such consult that Scripture, "As often as ye eat this bread and drink this cup, ye show the Lord's death till He come," 1 Corinthians 11:26. The Lord's death is to be remembered sacramentally till He comes to judgment.

2. *See the misery of unbelievers.* Though the Lord has appointed this glorious ordinance of His body and blood, they reap no benefit by it. They come to the Sacrament either to keep up their credit or to stop the mouth of their conscience, but they get nothing for their souls. They come empty of grace and go away empty of comfort. "It shall even be as when a hungry man dreameth, and behold he eateth, but he awaketh, and his soul is empty," Isaiah 29:8. So wicked men fancy that they eat of this spiritual banquet, but they are in a golden dream. Alas, they do not discern the Lord's body. The manna lay round about Israel's camp, but they did not know it. "They wist not what it was," Exodus 16:15. So, carnal persons see the external elements, but Christ is not known to them in His saving virtues. There is honey in this spiritual rock which they never taste. They feed upon the bread, but not Christ in the bread. Isaac ate the kid when he thought it had been venison, Genesis 27:25. Unbelievers go away with the shadow of the Sacrament. They have the rind and

the husk, not the marrow. They eat the kid, not the
venison.

   3. *See in this text, as in a glass, infinite love displayed.*
      (1) Behold the love of God the Father in giv-
ing Christ to be broken for us. That God should put
such a jewel in pledge is the admiration of angels.
"God so loved the world that He gave His only begot-
ten Son," John 3:16. It is a pattern of love without a
parallel. It was a far greater expression of love in
God to give His Son to die for us than if He had vol-
untarily acquitted us of the debt without any satisfaction at all. If a subject is disloyal to his sovereign, it
argues more love in the king to give his own son to
die for that subject than to forgive him the wrong
freely.
      (2) That Christ should suffer death. "Lord,"
said Bernard, "Thou hast loved me more than
Thyself; for Thou didst lay down Thy life for me."
The emperor Trajan rent off a piece of his own robe
to bind up one of his soldier's wounds. Christ rent
off His own flesh for us. Nay, that Christ should die
as the greatest sinner, having the weight of all
men's sins laid upon Him, here was most transport-
ing love! It sets all the angels in heaven wondering.
      (3) That Christ should die freely. "I lay down
My life," John 10:17. There was no law to enjoin
Him, no force to compel Him. It is called the offering of the body of Jesus, Hebrews 10:10. What could
fasten Him to the cross but the golden link of love!
      (4) That Christ should die for such as we are.
What are we? Not only vanity, but enmity! When we
were fighting, He was dying. When He had the

weapons in our hands, then He had the spear in His side, Romans 5:8.

(5) That Christ died for us when He could not expect to be at all bettered by us. We were reduced to penury. We were in such a condition that we could neither merit Christ's love nor requite it. For Christ to die for us when we were at such a low ebb was the very quintessence of love. One man will extend kindness to another as long as he is able to requite him. But if he is fallen to decay, then love begins to slacken and cool. But when we were engulfed in misery and fallen to decay, when we had lost our beauty, stained our blood, and spent our portion, then Christ died for us. O amazing love, which may swallow up all our thoughts!

(6) That Christ should not repent of His sufferings. "He shall see the travail of His soul and shall be satisfied," Isaiah 53:11. It is a metaphor that alludes to a mother who, though she has suffered greatly, does not repent of it when she sees a child brought forth. So, though Christ had hard travail upon the cross, yet He does not repent of it, but thinks all His sufferings well-bestowed. He shall be satisfied. The Hebrew word signifies such a satiating as a man has at some sweet repast or banquet.

(7) That Christ should rather die for us than the angels that fell. They were creatures of a more noble extraction and, in all probability, might have brought greater revenues of glory to God. Yet, that Christ should pass by those golden vessels and make us clods of earth into stars of glory, O the hyperbole of Christ's love!

(8) Yet another step of Christ's love, for like

the waters of the sanctuary it rises higher: that Christ's love should not cease at the hour of death! We write in our letters, "your friend till death." But Christ wrote in another style, "your Friend after death!" Christ died once, but loves forever. He is not testifying His affection to us. He is making the mansions ready for us, John 14:2. He is interceding for us, Hebrews 7:25. He appears in the court as the Advocate for the client. When He has finished dying, yet He has not finished loving. What a stupendous love was here! Who can meditate upon this and not be in ecstasy? Well may the apostle call it "a love that passes knowledge," Ephesians 3:19. When you see Christ broken in the Sacrament, think of this love.

4. *See, then, what dear and entire affections we should bear to Christ, who gives us His body and blood in the eucharist.* If He had had anything to part with of more worth, He would have bestowed it upon us. O let Christ lie nearest our hearts! Let Him be our Tree of Life, and let us desire no other fruit. Let Him be our morning Star, and let us rejoice in no other light. As Christ's beauty, so His bounty should make Him loved by us. He has given us His blood as the price and His Spirit as the witness of our pardon. In the Sacrament, Christ bestows all good things. He both imputes His righteousness and imparts His lovingkindness. He gives a foretaste of that supper which shall be celebrated in the paradise of God. To sum up all, in the blessed supper, Christ gives Himself to believers, and what can He give more? Dear Savior, how should Thy name be as ointment poured

forth! The Persians worship the sun for their god. Let us worship the Sun of righteousness. Though Judas sold Christ for 30 pieces, let us rather part with all than this pearl. Christ is that golden pipe through which the golden oil of salvation is transmitted to us.

Was Christ's body broken? Then we may behold sin odious in the red glass of Christ's sufferings. It is true, sin is to be abominated since it turned Adam out of paradise and threw the angels down to hell. Sin is the peace-breaker. It is like an incendiary in the family that sets husband and wife at variance. It makes God fall out with us. Sin is the birthplace of our sorrows and the grave of our comforts. But that which may most of all disfigure the face of sin and make it appear abominable is this: It crucified our Lord! It made Christ veil His glory and lose His blood.

If a woman saw the sword that killed her husband, how hateful would the sight of it be to her! Do we count that sin light which made Christ's soul heavy unto death? Mark 14:34. Can that be our joy which made the Lord Jesus a man of sorrows? Isaiah 53:3. Did He cry out, "My God, why hast Thou forsaken Me?" And shall not those sins be forsaken by us which made Christ Himself forsaken? O let us look upon sin with indignation! When a temptation comes to sin, let us say, as David, "Is not this the blood of the men that went in jeopardy of their lives?" 2 Samuel 23:17. So is not this the sin that poured out Christ's blood? Let our hearts be enraged against sin. When the senators of Rome showed the people Caesar's bloody robe, they were incensed against those that slew Him. Sin has rent the white robe of Christ's flesh and died it a crimson color. Let us, then, seek to be avenged of our sins. Under the Law, if an ox gored a man so that he died, the ox was to be killed, Exodus 21:28. Sin has gored and pierced our Savior. Let it die the death. What a pity is it for that to live which would not suffer Christ to live!

Was Christ's body broken? Let us, then, from His suffering on the cross, learn this lesson not to wonder much if we meet with troubles in the world. Did Christ suffer who "knew no sin," and do we think it strange to suffer who know nothing *but* sin? Did Christ feel the anger of God? And is it much for us to feel the anger of men? Was the Head crowned with thorns? Must we have our bracelets and diamonds when Christ had the spear and nails going to His heart? Truly, such as are guilty may well expect the lash when He, who was innocent, could not go free.

USE 3. The third use is of exhortation, and it has several branches.

BRANCH 1. Was Christ's body broken for us? Let us be affected with the great goodness of Christ. Who can tread upon these hot coals and his heart not burn? Cry out with Ignatius, "Christ, my love, is crucified." If a friend should die for us, would not our hearts be much affected with his kindness? That the God of heaven should die for us, how should this stupendous mercy have a melting influence upon us! The body of Christ broken is enough to break the most flinty heart. At our Savior's passion, the very stones cleaved asunder. "The rocks rent," Matthew 27:51. He who is not affected with this has a heart harder than the stones. If Saul was so affected with David's mercy in sparing his life, 1 Samuel 24:16, how may we be affected with Christ's kindness who, to spare our life, lost His own! Let us pray that, as Christ was *crucifixus,* so He may be *cordi-fixus.* That is, as He was fastened to the cross, so He may be fasted to our hearts.

BRANCH 2. Is Jesus Christ spiritually exhibited to us in the Sacrament? Let us then set a high value and estimate upon Him.

Let us prize Christ's body. Every crumb of this Bread of life is precious. "My flesh is meat indeed," John 6:55. The manna was a lively type and emblem of Christ's body, for manna was sweet. "The taste of it was like wafers made with honey," Exodus 16:31. It was a delicious food. Therefore it was called angel's fod for its excellency. So Christ, the sacramental manna, is sweet to a believer's soul. "His fruit was sweet to my taste," Song of Solomon 2:3. Everything of Christ is sweet. His name is sweet. His virtue is sweet. This manna sweetens the waters of Marah.

Nay, Christ's flesh excels manna. Manna was food, but not medicine. If an Israelite had been sick, manna could not have cured him. But this blessed manna of Christ's body is not only for food but for medicine. Christ has healing under His wings, Malachi 4:2. He heals the blind eye, the hard heart. Take this medicine next to your heart and it will heal you of all your spiritual distempers. Also, manna was corruptible. It ceased when Israel came to Canaan. But this blessed manna of Christ's body will never cease. The saints will feed with infinite delight and soul satisfaction upon Christ to all eternity. The joys of heaven would cease if this manna should cease. The manna was put in a golden pot in the ark to be preserved there. So the blessed manna of Christ's body, being put in the golden pot of the Divine nature, is laid up in the ark of heaven for the support of saints forever. Well, then, may we say of Christ's blessed body, it is meat indeed. In the field of Christ's body, being digged upon the cross, we find the pearl of salvation.

Let us prize Christ's blood in the Sacrament. It is drink indeed, John 6:55. Here is the nectar and ambrosia God Himself delights to taste of. This is both a balsam and a perfume.

SEVEN SUPERNATURAL VIRTUES IN CHRIST'S BLOOD

That we may set the higher value upon the blood of Christ. I shall show you seven rare supernatural virtues in it:

1. It is a reconciling blood. "You that were sometime alienated, and enemies, yet now hath He reconciled through death," Colossians 1:21. Christ's blood is the blood of atonement. Nay, it is not only a sacrifice but a propitiation, 1 John 2:2, which denotes a bringing us into favor with God. It is one thing for a traitor to be pardoned, and another thing to be brought into favor. Sin rent us off from God; Christ's blood cements us to God. If we had had as much grace as the angels, it could not have

wrought our reconciliation. If we had offered up millions of holocausts and sacrifices, if we had wept rivers of tears, this could never have appeased an angry Deity. Only Christ's blood ingratiates us into God's favor and makes Him look upon us with a smiling aspect. When Christ died, the veil of the temple was rent. This was not without a mystery, to show that through Christ's blood the veil of our sins is rent which interposed between God and us.

2. Christ's blood is a quickening blood. "Whoso drinketh My blood, hath eternal life," John 6:54. It both begets life and prevents death. "The life of a thing is in the blood," Leviticus 17:11. Sure enough, the life of our soul is in the blood of Christ. When we contract deadness of heart, and are like wine that has lost the spirits, Christ's blood has an elevating power; it puts vivacity into us, making us quick and lively in our motion. "They shall mount up with wings as eagles," Isaiah 40:31.

3. Christ's blood is a cleansing blood. "How much more shall the blood of Christ purge your conscience!" Hebrews 9:14. As the merit of Christ's blood pacifies God, so the virtue of it purifies us. It is the King of heaven's bath. It is a laver to wash in. It washes a crimson sinner milk white. "The blood of Jesus cleanseth us from all our sin," 1 John 1:7. The Word of God is a looking glass to show us our spots, and the blood of Christ is a fountain to wash them away, Zechariah 13:1.

But this blood will not wash if it is mingled with anything. If we go to mingle anything with Christ's blood, either the merits of saints or the prayers of angels, it will not wash. Let Christ's blood be pure and unmixed, and there is no spot but it will wash away. It purged out Noah's drunkenness and Lot's incest. Indeed, there is one spot so black that Christ's blood does not wash away, and that is the sin against the Holy Ghost. Not but that there is virtue enough in Christ's blood to wash it away, but he who has sinned that sin will not be washed. He condemns Christ's blood and tramples it under foot, Hebrews 10:29.

4. Christ's blood is a softening blood. There is nothing so hard but may be softened by this blood. It will soften a stone. Water will soften the earth, but it will not soften a stone; but Christ's blood mollifies a stone. It softens a heart of stone. It turns a flint into a spring. The heart, which before was like a piece hewn out of a rock, being steeped in Christ's blood, becomes soft and the waters of repentance flow from it. How was the jailer's heart dissolved and made tender when the blood of sprinkling was upon it! "Sirs, what must I do to be saved?" Acts 16:30. His heart was now like melting wax. God might set what seal and impression He would upon it.

5. Christ's blood cools the heart. First, it cools the heart of sin. The heart naturally is full of distempered heat. It must be hot, being set on fire of hell. It burns in lust and passion. Christ's blood allays this heart and quenches the enflammation of sin. Second, it cools the heat of conscience. It times of desertion, conscience burns with the heat of God's displeasure. Now, Christ's blood, being sprinkled upon the conscience, cools and pacifies it. And, in this sense, Christ is compared to a river of water, Isaiah 32:2. When the heart burns and is in agony,

Christ's blood is like water to the fire. It has a cooling, refreshing virtue in it.

6. Christ's blood comforts the soul. It is good against fainting fits. Christ's blood is better than wine. Though wine cheers the heart of a man who is well, yet it will not cheer his heart when he has a fit of the stone or when the pangs of death are upon him. But Christ's blood will cheer the heart at such a time. It is best in affliction. It cures the trembling of the heart.

A conscience sprinkled with Christ's blood can, like the nightingale, sing with a thorn at its breast. The blood of Christ can make a prison become a palace. It turned the martyr's flames into beds of roses. Christ's blood gives comfort at the hour of death. As a holy man once said on his deathbed when they brought him a cordial, "No cordial like the blood of Christ!"

7. Christ's blood procures heaven. Israel passed through the Red Sea to Canaan. So, through the red sea of Christ's blood, we enter into the heavenly Canaan. "Having boldness therefore to enter into the holiest by the blood of Jesus," Hebrews 10:19. Our sins shut heaven; Christ's blood is the key which opens the gate of paradise for us. Hence it is that Theodoret calls the cross the tree of salvation because that blood which trickled down the cross distils salvation. Well, then, may we prize the blood of Christ and, with Paul, determine to know nothing but Christ crucified, 1 Corinthians 2:2. King's crowns are only crosses, but the cross of Christ is the only crown.

BRANCH 3. Does Christ offer His body and blood to us in the Supper? Then with what solemn preparation should we come to so sacred an ordinance! It is not enough to do *what* God has appointed, but *as* He has appointed. "Prepare your hearts unto the Lord," 1 Samuel 7:3. The musician first puts his instrument in tune before he plays. The heart must be prepared and put in tune before it goes to meet with God in this solemn ordinance of the Sacrament. Take heed of rashness and irreverence. If we do not come prepared, we do not drink but spill Christ's blood. "Whosoever shall eat this bread and drink this cup of the Lord unworthily, shall be guilty of the body and blood of the Lord," 1 Corinthians 11:27. That is, said Theophylact, he shall be judged a shedder of Christ's blood. We read of a wine cup of fury in God's hand, Jeremiah 25:15. He that comes unprepared to the Lord's Supper turns the cup in the Sacrament into a cup of fury.

Oh, with what reverence and devotion should we address ourselves to these holy mysteries! The saints are called "prepared vessels," Romans 9:23. If ever these vessels should be prepared, it is when they are to hold the precious body and blood of Christ. The sinner who is damned is first prepared. Men do not go to hell without some kind of preparation. "Vessels fitted for destruction," Romans 9:22. If those vessels are prepared which are filled with wrath, much more are those to be prepared who are to receive Christ in the Sacrament. Let us dress ourselves by a Scripture glass before we come to the Lord's Table and, with the Lamb's wife, make ourselves ready.

HOW SHOULD WE PREPARE FOR
THE LORD'S SUPPER?

1. *We must come with self-examining hearts.* "But let a man examine himself, and so let him eat of that bread," 1 Corinthians 11:28. It is not enough that others think we are fit to come, but we must examine ourselves. The Greek word "to examine" is a metaphor taken from the goldsmith who curiously tries his metals. So before we come to the Lord's Table, we are to make a curious and critical trial of ourselves by the Word.

Self-examination, being a reflexive act, is difficult. It is hard for a man to look inward and see the face of his own soul. The eye can see everything but itself.

But this work is necessary because, if we do not examine ourselves, we are at a loss about our spiritual estate. We know not whether we are interested in the covenant or whether we have a right to the seal. Also, because God will examine us. It was a sad question the master of the feast asked, "Friend, how camest thou in hither, not having a wedding garment?" Matthew 22:12. So it will be terrible when God shall say to a man, "How did you come in here to My table with a proud, vain, unbelieving heart? What have you to do here in your sins. You pollute My holy things."

What need, therefore, is there to make a heart search before we come to the Lord's Supper! We should examine our sins that they may be mortified, our wants that they may be supplied, our graces that they may be strengthened.

2. *We must come with serious hearts.* Our spirits are feathery and light, like a vessel without ballast, which floats in the water but does not sail. We float in holy duties and are full of vain excursions, even when we are to deal with God and are engaged in matters of life and death. That which may consolidate our hearts and make them fix with seriousness is to consider that God's eye is now especially upon us when we approach His table. "The king came in to see the guests," Matthew 22:11. God knows every communicant, and if He sees any levity and indecency of spirit in us, in worthy of His presence, He will be highly incensed and send us away with the guilt of Christ's blood instead of the comfort of it.

3. *We must come with intelligent hearts.* There ought to be a competent measure of knowledge, that we may discern the Lord's body. As we are to pray with understanding, 1 Corinthians 14:15, so ought we to communicate at the Lord's Table with understanding. If knowledge is lacking, it cannot be a reasonable service, Romans 12:1. They that do not know the mystery do not feel the comfort. We must know God the Father in His attributes, God the Son in His offices, God the Holy Ghost in His graces. Some say they have good hearts, yet lack knowledge. We may as well call that a good eye which lacks sight.

4. *We must come to the Sacrament with longing hearts.* Say as Christ, "With desire I have desired to eat of this passover," Luke 22:15. If God prepares a feast, we must get an appetite. Why has the Lord frowned

upon His people of late but to punish their surfeit and provoke their appetite? As David longed for the water of the well of Bethlehem, 2 Samuel 23:15, so should we long for Christ in the Sacrament. Desires are the sails of the soul which are spread to receive the gale of a heavenly blessing. For the exciting of holy desires and longings, consider:

(1) The magnificence and royalty of this supper. It is a heavenly banquet. "In this mountain shall the Lord of Hosts make unto all people a feast of fat things, a feast of wines on the lees," Isaiah 25:6. Here is the juice of that grape which comes from the true Vine. Under these elements of bread and wine, Christ and all His benefits are exhibited to us. The Sacrament is a repository and storehouse of celestial blessings. Behold here, life and peace and salvation set before us! All the sweet delicacies of heaven are served in this feast.

(2) To provoke appetite, consider what need we have of this spiritual repast. The angel persuaded Elijah to take a little of the cake and jar of water that he might not faint in his journey. "Arise and eat, because the journey is too great for thee," 1 Kings 19:7. So truly we have a great journey from earth to heaven. Therefore, we need to recruit ourselves by the way. How many sins have we to subdue! How many duties to perform! How many wants to supply! How many graces to strengthen! How many adversaries to conflict with! So that we need refreshment by the way. By feeding upon the body and blood of the Lord, we renew our strength as the eagle.

(3) Consider Christ's readiness to dispense divine blessings in this ordinance. Jesus Christ is

not a sealing fountain but a flowing fountain. It is but crying, and He gives us food. It is but thirsting, and He opens the conduit. "Let him that is athirst come; and whosoever will, let him take the water of life freely," Revelation 22:17. As the clouds have natural proneness to drop down their moisture upon the earth, so has Christ to give forth of His gracious virtues and influences to the soul.

(4) There is no danger of excess at this supper. Other feasts often cause gluttony; it is not so here. The more we take of the Bread of life, the more healthful we are and the more we come to our spiritual complexion. Fullness here does not increase humours, but comforts. In spiritual things there is no extreme. Though a drop of Christ's blood is sweet, yet the more, the better—the deeper, the sweeter. "Drink abundantly, O beloved," Song of Solomon 5:1.

(5) We do not know how long this feast may last. While the manna is to be had, let us bring our baskets. God will not always be spreading the cloth. If people lose their appetite, He will call to the enemy to take them away.

(6) Feeding upon Christ sacramentally will be a good preparation to sufferings. The Bread of life will help us to feed upon the bread of affliction. The cup of blessing will enable us to drink of the cup of persecution. Christ's blood is a wine that has a flavor in it and is full of spirits. Therefore, Cyprian tells us, when the primitive Christians were to appear before the cruel tyrants, they were wont to receive the Sacrament, and then they arose up from the Lord's Table as lions breathing forth the fire of heavenly

courage. Let these considerations be as sauce to sharpen our appetites to the Lord's Table. God loves to see us feed hungrily upon the Bread of life.

5. *If we would come prepared to this ordinance, we must come with penitent hearts.* The passover was to be eaten with bitter herbs. We must bring our myrrh of repentance which, though it is bitter to us, is sweet to Christ. "They shall look upon Me whom they have pierced and mourn for Him," Zechariah 12:10. A broken Christ is to be received with a broken heart. We that have sinned with Peter should weep with Peter. Our eyes should be filled with tears and our hearts steeped in the brinish waters of repentance. Say, "Lord Jesus, though I cannot bring sweet spices, and perfume Thy body as Mary did, yet I will wash Thy feet with my tears." The more bitterness we taste in sin, the more sweetness we shall taste in Christ.

6. *We must come with sincere hearts.* The tribes of Israel, being straitened in time, wanted some legal purifications. Yet because their hearts were sincere and they came with desire to meet with God in the Passover, therefore the Lord healed the people, 2 Chronicles 30:19-20. Bad aims will spoil good actions. An archer may miss the mark as well by squinting as by shooting short. What is our design in coming to the Sacrament? Is it that we may have more victory over our corruptions and be more confirmed in holiness? Then God will be good to us and heal us. Sincerity, like true gold, shall have some grains allowed for its lightness.

7. *We must come with hearts fired with love to Christ.* The spouse said, "I am sick of love," Song of Solomon 2:5. Let us give Christ the wine of our love to drink and weep that we can love Him no more. Would we have Christ's exhilarating presence in the supper? Let us meet Him with strong endearments of affection. Basil compares love to a sweet ointment. Christ delights to smell this perfume. The disciple that loved most, Christ put in His bosom.

8. *We must come with humble hearts.* We see Christ humbling Himself to death. And will a humble Christ ever be received into a proud heart? A sight of God's glory and a sight of sin may humble us. Was Christ humble, who was all purity? And are we proud, who are all leprosy? O let us come with a sense of our own vileness. How humble should he be who is to receive alms of free grace? Jesus Christ is a lily of the valley, Song of Solomon 2:1, not of the mountains. Humility was never a loser. The emptier the vessel is, and the lower it is let down into the well, the more water it draws up. So the more the soul is emptied of itself, and the lower it is let down by humility, the more it fetches out of the well of salvation. God will come into a humble heart to revive it, Isaiah 57:15. That is none of Christ's temple which is not built with a low roof.

9. *We must come with heavenly hearts.* The mystery of the Sacrament is heavenly. What should an earthworm do here? He is not likely to feed on Christ's body and blood who, with the serpent, eats dust. The Sacrament is called "communion," 1 Corinthians

10:16. What communion can earthly man have with Christ? First, there must be conformity before communion. He that is earthly is no more conformed in likeness to Christ than a clod of dust is like a star. An earthly man makes the world his god. Then let him not think to receive another God in the Sacrament. O let us be in the heavenly altitudes and, by the wing of grace, ascend!

10. *We must come with believing hearts.* Christ gave the Sacrament to the apostles, principally as they were believers. Such as come faithless go away fruitless. Nor it is enough to have the habit of faith. We must exert and put forth the vigorous actings of faith in this ordinance.

(1) Let us exercise the eye of faith. Faith has an eagle's eye. It pierces into things far remote from sense. Faith takes a prospect of heaven. It discerns Him who is invisible, Hebrews 11:27. It beholds a beauty and fulness in Christ. It sees this beauty shining through the lattice of an ordinance. Faith views Christ's love streaming in His blood. Look upon Christ with believing eyes and you shall, one day, see Him with glorified eyes.

(2) Exercise the mouth of faith. Here is the bread broken. What use is there of bread but to feed on? Feed upon the Bread of God. Adam died by eating; we live by eating. In the Sacrament, the whole Christ is presented to us, the Divine and the human nature. All kind of virtue comes from Him, mortifying, mollifying, comforting. Oh, then, feed on Him! This grace of faith is the great grace to be set on work at the Sacrament.

QUESTION. But does the virtue lie simply in faith?

ANSWER. Not in faith considered purely as a grace, but as it has respect to the object. The virtue is not in faith, but in Christ. Consider this: A ring which has a precious stone in it which will staunch blood. We say that the ring staunches blood, but it is the stone in the ring. So faith is the ring, Christ is the precious stone. All that faith does is to bring home Christ's merits to the soul, and so it justifies. The virtue is not in faith but in Christ.

QUESTION. But why should faith carry away more from Christ in the Sacrament than any other grace?

ANSWER 1. Because faith is the most receptive grace. It is the receiving of gold which enriches. So faith, receiving Christ's merits and filling the soul with all the fulness of God, must be an enriching grace. In the body, there are veins that suck the nourishment which comes into the stomach and turns it into blood and spirits. Faith is such a sucking vein that draws virtue from Christ. Therefore it is called a precious faith, 2 Peter 1:1.

ANSWER 2. Faith has more of Christ's benefits annexed to it because it is the most humble grace. If repentance should fetch justification from Christ, a man would be ready to say, "This was for my tears." But faith is humble; it is an empty hand, and what merit can there be in that? Does a poor man, reaching out his hand, merit an alms? So because faith is humble, and gives all the glory to Christ and free grace, hence it is that God has put so much honor

on it. This shall be the grace to which Christ and all
His merits belong. Therefore, above all graces, set
faith to work in the Sacrament. Faith fetches in all
provisions. This is the golden bucket that draws water out of the well of life.

But there is a bastard faith in the world. Pliny
tells of a Cyprian stone which is, in color and splendor, like the diamond, but it is not of the right kind.
It will break with the hammer. So, there is a false
faith which sparkles and makes a show in the eye of
the world, but it is not genuine; it will break with
the hammer of persecution.

Six Differences Between a Sincere Faith and a Hypocritical Faith

Therefore, to prevent mistakes, and that we may
not be deceived and think we believe when we only
presume, I shall give you six differences between a
sincere faith, which is the flower of the spirit, and a
hypocritical faith, which is the fruit of fancy.

1. A hypocritical faith is easy to come by. It is like
the seed in the parable which sprung up suddenly,
Mark 4:5. A false faith shoots up without any convictions and soul humblings. As Isaac said, "How
comest thou by thy venison so soon?" Genesis 27:20.
Likewise, how does this man come by faith so soon?
Surely it is of different nature and will quickly wither
away. But true faith, being an an outlandish plant
and of a heavenly extraction, is hard to come by. It
costs many a sigh and tear, Acts 2:37. This spiritual
infant is not born without pangs.

2. A hypocritical faith is afraid to come to trial.

The hypocrite would rather have his faith commended than examined. He can no more endure a Scripture trial than counterfeit metal can endure the touchstone. He is like a man who has stolen goods in his house and is very unwilling to have his house searched. So the hypocrite has gotten some stolen goods that the devil has helped him to, and he is loathe to have his heart searched. Whereas true faith is willing to come to a trial. "Examine me, O Lord, and prove me; try my reins and heart," Psalm 26:2. David was not afraid to be tried by a jury, no, though God Himself was one of the jury. Good wares are never afraid of the light.

3. A hypocritical faith has a slight esteem of true faith. The hypocrite hears others speak in the commendation of faith, but he wonders where the virtue of it lies. He looks upon faith as a drug, or some base commodity that will not go off. He will part with all the faith he has for a piece of silver and, perhaps, it might be dear enough at the price. But the man who has true faith sets a high value on it. He reckons this grace among his jewels. What incorporates him into Christ but faith? What puts him into a state of sonship but faith? Galatians 3:26. O precious faith! A believer would not exchange his shield of faith for a crown of gold!

4. A hypocritical faith is lame on one hand. With one hand it would take up Christ. But it does not with the other hand give itself up to Christ. It would take Christ by way of surety, but not give up itself to Him by way of surrender. True faith, however, is impartial. It takes Christ as a Savior and submits to Him as a Prince. Christ said, "With My body and My

blood, I endow thee." And faith says, "With my soul, I
worship Thee."

5. A hypocritical faith is impure. The hypocrite
says he believes, yet goes on in sin. He is all creed,
but no commandment. He believes, yet will take
God's name in vain. "Wilt thou not cry unto me, My
Father, thou art the guide of my youth! Behold, thou
hast done evil things as thou couldst," Jeremiah
3:4-5. These impostors would call God their Father,
yet sin as fast as they could. For one to say he has
faith, yet live in sin, is as if a man should say he was
in health, yet his vitals had perished. But a true faith
is joined with sanctity. "Holding the mystery of faith
in a pure conscience," 1 Timothy 3:9. The jewel of
faith is always put in the cabinet of a good conscience. The woman who touched Christ by faith felt
a healing virtue come from Him. Though faith does
not wholly remove sin, yet it subdues it.

6. A hypocritical faith is a dead faith; it tastes no
sap or sweetness in Christ. The hypocrite tastes
something in the vine and olive. He finds contentment in the carnal, luscious delights of the world,
but no sweetness in a promise. The Holy Ghost
Himself is spiritless to him. That is a dead faith
which has no sense or taste. But true faith finds
much delight in heavenly things. The Word is
sweeter than the honeycomb, Psalm 19:10. Christ's
love is better than wine, Song of Solomon 1:2. Thus
we see a difference between true and spurious faith.
How many have thought they have had the live child
of faith by them, when it has proved the dead child.
Take heed of presumption, but cherish faith. Faith
applies Christ and makes a spiritual concoction of

His body and blood. This supper was intended chiefly for believers, Luke 22:19. Christ's blood to an unbeliever is like *aqua-vitae* in a dead man's mouth: it loses all its virtue.

11.* *We must come to the Lord's Table with charitable hearts.* "Purge out, therefore, the old leaven," 1 Corinthians 5:7. The leaven of malice will sour the ordinance to us. We must come with bitter tears, yet not with bitter spirits. The Lord's Supper is a love feast. Christ's blood was shed not only to reconcile us to God but to one another. Christ's body was broken to make up the breaches among Christians. How sad is it that they who profess they are going to eat Christ's flesh in the Sacrament should tear the flesh of one another! "Whosoever hateth his brother is a murderer," 1 John 3:15. He who comes to the Lord's Table in hatred is a Judas to Christ and a Cain to his brother. What benefit can he receive at the Sacrament whose heart is poisoned with malice?

If one drinks poison and immediately takes medicine, surely the medicine will do him no good. Such as are poisoned with rancour and malice are not the better for the sacramental medicine. He that does not come in charity to the sacrament has nothing of God in him, for "God is love," 1 John 4:16. He knows nothing of the gospel savingly, for it is a gospel of peace, Ephesians 6:15. He has none of the wisdom which comes from heaven, for that is gentle and easy to be entreated, James 3:17. Oh, that Christians were rooted and cemented together in love!

---

* This point follows point 10 from page 135.

Shall devils unite and saints divide? Did we thus learn Christ? Has not the Lord Jesus loved us to the death? What greater reproach can be cast upon such a loving Head than for the members to smite one against another? The good Lord put out the fire of contention and kindles the fire of love and amity in all our hearts.

12. *We must come with praying hearts.* Every ordinance, as well as every creature, is sanctified by prayer, 1 Timothy 4:5. Prayer turns the element into spiritual aliment. When we send the dove of prayer to heaven, it brings an olive leaf in its mouth. We should pray that God would enrich His ordinance with His presence; that He would make the Sacrament effectual to all those holy ends and purposes for which He has appointed it; that it may be the feast of our graces and the funeral of our corruptions; that it may be not only a sign to represent, but an instrument to convey Christ to us, and a seal to assure us of our heavenly union. If we would have the fat and sweet of this ordinance, we must send prayer before, as a harbinger, to bespeak a blessing.

Some are so distracted with worldly cares that they can scarcely spare any time for prayer before they come to the Sacrament. Do they think the tree of blessing will drop its fruit into their mouth when they never shook it by prayer? God does not set His mercies at so low a rate as to cast them away upon those who do not seek them, Ezekiel 36:37.

Nor is it enough to pray, but it must be with heat and intensity of soul. Jacob wrestled in prayer, Genesis 32:24. Cold prayers, like cold suitors, never speed. Prayer must be with sighs and groans, Romans 8:26. It must be in the Holy Ghost, Jude 20. He who will speak to God, said St. Ambrose, must speak to Him in His own language which He understands, that is, in the language of His Spirit.

13. *We must come to the Lord's Table with self-denying hearts.* When we have prepared ourselves in the best manner we can, let us take heed of trusting our preparations. "When ye shall have done all these things which are commanded you, say, We are unprofitable servants," Luke 17:15. Use duty, but do not idolize it. We ought to use duties to fit us for Christ, but we must not make a Christ of our duties. Duty is the golden path to walk in, but not a silver crutch to lean on. Alas! What are all our preparations? God can spy a hole in our best garments. "All our righteousness is as filthy rags," Isaiah 64:6. When we have prepared ourselves as hoping in God's mercy, we must deny ourselves as deserving His justice. If our holiest services are not sprinkled with Christ's blood, they are no better than shining sins and, like Uriah's letter, they carry in them the matter of our death. Use duty, but trust Christ and free grace for acceptance. Be like Noah's dove. She made use of her wings to fly, but trust in the ark for safety.

We see how we are to be qualified in our addresses to the Lord's Table. Thus coming, we shall meet with embraces of mercy. We shall have not only a representation but a participation of Christ in the Sacrament. We shall be filled with all the fulness of God, Ephesians 3:19.

BRANCH 4.* Has Jesus Christ made this gospel banquet? Is He both the founder and the feast? Then let poor, doubting Christians be encouraged to come to the Lord's Table. Satan would hinder from the Sacrament, as Saul hindered the people from eating honey, 1 Samuel 14:26. But is there any soul that has been humbled and bruised for sin, whose heart secretly pants after Christ, but yet stands trembling and dares not approach to these holy mysteries? Let me encourage that soul to come. "Arise, He calleth thee," Mark 10:49.

OBJECTION 1. But I am sinful and unworthy, and why should I meddle with such holy things?

ANSWER. Who did Christ die for but such? "He came into the world to save sinners," 1 Timothy 1:15. He took our sins upon Him as well as our nature. "He bare our griefs," Isaiah 53:4. In the Hebrew it is "our sicknesses." See your sins, said Luther, upon Christ, and then they are no more yours but His. Our sins should humble us, but they must not discourage us from coming to Christ. The more diseased we are, the rather we should step into this pool of Siloam. Who does Christ invite to the supper but the poor, halted, and maimed? Luke 14:21—that is, such as see themselves unworthy and fly to Christ for sanctuary. The priest was to take a bunch of hyssop, dip it in blood, and sprinkle it upon the leper, Leviticus 14:6-7. You who have the leprosy of sin upon you, yet if, as a leper, you loathe yourself, Christ's precious blood shall be sprinkled upon you.

---

* Branch 4 follows Branch 3 from page 128.

OBJECTION 2. But I have sinned presumptuously against mercy. I have contracted guilt after I have been at the Lord's Table, and surely Christ's blood is not for me.

ANSWER. It is, indeed, grievous to abuse mercy. It was the aggravation of Solomon's sin. His heart was turned from the Lord "who had appeared to him twice," 1 Kings 11:9. Presumptuous sins open the mouth of conscience to accuse and shut the mouth of God's Spirit, which should speak peace. Yet do not cast away your anchor. Look up to the blood of Christ. It can forgive sins against mercy. Did not Noah sin against mercy, who, though he had been so miraculously perserved in the flood, yet soon after he came out of the ark was drunk? Did not David sin against mercy when, after God had made him king, he stained his soul with lust and his robe with blood? Yet both these sins were washed away in that fountain which is set open for Judah to wash in, Zechariah 13:1.

Did not the disciples deal unkindly with Christ in the time of His suffering? Peter denied him, and all the rest fled from his colors. "Then all the disciples forsook Him and fled," Matthew 26:56. Yet Christ did not take advantage of their weakness, nor did He cast them off, but sends the joyful news of His resurrection to them, Matthew 27:7, and of His ascension. "Go to my brethren and say unto them, I ascend to My Father, and your Father," John 20:17. And, lest Peter should think he was none of the number that should be interested in Christ's love, therefore Christ dispatched away a special message to Peter to comfort him. "Go tell the disciples and

Peter, that He goes before you into Galilee, there shall ye see Him," Mark 16:7. So that where our hearts are sincere and our turnings aside are rather from a defect in our power than our will, the Lord Jesus will not take advantage of every failing. Instead He will drop His blood upon us, which has a voice in it which speaks better things than the blood of Abel, Hebrews 12:24.

OJBECTION 3. But I find such a faintness and feebleness in my soul that I dare not go to the Lord's Table.

ANSWER. You have all the more need to go. Drink of this wine for your infirmities, 1 Timothy 5:23. Would it not be strange for a man to argue thus: "My body is weak and declining; therefore, I will not go to the physician." He should the rather go! Our weakness should send us to Christ. His blood is mortal to sin and vital to grace. You say you have defects in your soul. If you had none, there would be no need of a Mediator, nor would Christ have any work to do. Oh, therefore, turn your disputing into believing. Be encouraged to come to this blessed supper. You shall find Christ giving forth His sweet influences and your grace shall flourish as an herb.

OBJECTION 4. But I have often come to this ordinance and found no fruit. I am not filled with comfort.

ANSWER. God may meet you in an ordinance when you do not discern it. Christ was with Mary, yet she did not know it was Christ. You think Christ has not met you at His table because he does not give you comfort.

Though He does not fill you with comfort, He may fill you with strength. We think we have no answer from God in a duty unless He fills us with joy. Yet God may manifest His presence as well by giving strength as comfort. If we have power from heaven to foil our corruptions and to walk more closely and evenly with God, this is an answer from God. "I will strengthen them in the Lord," Zechariah 10:12. If, Christian, you do not have God's arm to embrace you, yet if you have His arm to strengthen you, this is the fruit of an ordinance.

If God does not fill your heart with joy, yet if He fills your eyes with tears, this is His meeting you at His table. When you look upon Christ broken on the cross, and consider His love and your ingratitude, this makes the dew begin to fall, and your eyes are like the fish pools in Heshbon, full of water, Song of Solomon 7:4. This is God's graciously meeting with you in the Sacrament. Bless His name for it. It is a sign the Sun of righteousness has risen upon us, when our frozen hearts melt in tears for sin.

If your comforts are low, yet if the actings of your faith are high, this is God's manifesting His presence in the supper. The sensible tokens of God's love are withheld, but the soul ventures on Christ's blood. It believes that, coming to Him, He will hold out the golden sceptre, John 6:37. This glorious acting of faith, and the inward quiet that faith breeds, is the blessed return of an ordinance. "He will turn again, He will have compassion on us," Micah 7:19. The church's comforts were darkened, but her faith

breaks forth as the sun out of a cloud. He will have
compassion on us. This acting of faith makes us in a
blessed condition. "Blessed are they which have not
seen, yet have believed," John 20:29.

OBJECTION 5. But I cannot find any of these
things in the Sacrament. My heart is dead and
locked up and I have no return at all.

ANSWER. Wait on God for an answer of the ordinance. God has promised to fill the soul. "He fil-
leth the hungry soul with goodness," Psalm 107:9. If
not with gladness, yet with goodness. The soul must
be filled or how can the promise be fulfilled?
Christian! God has said it. Therefore wait. Will you
not believe God unless you have a voice from
heaven? The Lord has given you His promise. And is
it not as good security to have a bill under a man's
hand as to have it by word of mouth? Be content to
wait awhile, mercy will come. God's mercies in
Scripture are not called speedy mercies, but they are
called sure mercies, Isaiah 55:3.

BRANCH 5. Has Christ given us His body's
blood? Then when we are at this gospel ordinance,
let us remember the Lord Jesus there. The Sacrament is a Christ-remembering ordinance. "This do
in remembrance of Me," 1 Corinthians 11:25. God
has appointed this spiritual festival to preserve the
living memory of our dying Savior. A Sacrament-day
is a commemoration day.

Remember Christ's passion. "Remembering the
wormwood and the gall," Lamentations 3:19. I may
alter the words a little: "Remembering the vinegar

and the gall." If the manna was to be kept in the ark so that the memory of it should be preserved, how should the death and suffering of Christ be kept in our minds as a memorial when we are at the table of the Lord?

Remember the glorious benefits we receive from the broken body of Christ. We usually remember those things which are advantageous to us. Christ's broken body is a screen to keep off the fire of God's wrath from us. Christ's body being broken, the serpents head is broken. Christ being broken upon the cross, a box of precious jewels is broken open. Now we have access to God with boldness. The blood of the cross has made way to the throne of grace. Now we are made sons and heirs, and to be heir to the promise is better than to be heir to the crown. Christ having died, we are made near akin to the blessed Trinity. We are candidates and expectants of glory. The bloody way of the cross is our milky way to heaven. Jesus Christ drank gall that we might drink the honey streams of Canaan. His cross was stuck full of nails that our crown might be hung full of jewels. Well may we remember Christ in the blessed Sacrament!

But the bare remembrance of Christ's death is not enough. Some who have a natural tenderness of spirit may be affected with the history of Christ's passion, but this remembrance of Christ has little comfort in it. Let us remember Christ in the Sacrament rightly.

Let us remember Christ's death with joy. "God forbid that I should glory, save in the cross of our Lord Jesus Christ," Galatians 6:14. When we see

Christ in the Sacrament crucified before our eyes, we may behold Him in that posture as He was in upon the cross, stretching out His blessed arms to receive us. O what matter of triumph and acclamation is this! Though we remember our sins with grief, yet we should remember Christ's sufferings with joy. Let us weep for those sins which shed His blood, yet rejoice in that blood which washes away our sins.

Let us so remember Christ's death as to be conformed to His death. "That I may be conformable to His death," Philippians 3:10. Then we remember Christ's death rightly when we are dead with Him. Our pride and passion are dead. Christ's dying for us makes sin die in us. Then we rightly remember Christ's crucifixion when we are crucified with Him. We are dead to the pleasures and preferments of the world. "The world is crucified unto me, and I to the world," Galatians 6:14.

BRANCH 6. If Christ has given us this soul festival for the strengthening of grace, let us labor to feel some virtue flowing out of this ordinance to us. It would be strange if a man should receive no nourishment from his food. It is a discredit to this ordinance if we get no increase of grace. Shall leanness enter into our souls at a feast of fat things? Christ gives us His body and blood for the augmenting of faith. He expects that we should reap some profit and income, and that our weak, minute faith should flourish into a great faith. "O woman, great is thy faith," Matthew 15:28. It would be good to examine whether, after our frequent celebration of this holy supper, we have arrived at a great faith.

QUESTION. How may I know whether I have this great faith?

ANSWER. For the solution of this, I shall lay down six eminent signs of a great faith. And, if we can show any one of them, we have made a good proficiency at the Sacrament.

SIX SIGNS OF A GREAT FAITH

1. A great faith can trust God without a pledge. It can rely upon providence in the deficiency of outward supplies. "Although the fig tree shall not blossom, neither shall fruit be in the vines, the labor of the olive shall fail, yet will I rejoice in the Lord," Habakkuk 3:17-18. An unbeliever must have something to feed his senses or he gives up the ghost. When he is at his wealth's end, he is at his wit's end. Faith does not question but that God will provide, though it does not see which way provisions should come in. Faith does not fear famine. God has set His seal to it, "Verily thou shalt be fed," Psalm 37:3. Faith puts the bond in suit. "Lord," says faith, "wilt Thou feed the birds of the air, and wilt not Thou feed me? Shall I lack when my Father keeps the purse?" A good Christian with the rod of faith smites the Rock in heaven, and some honey and oil comes out for recruiting his present necessities.

2. A great faith is a wonder-working faith. It can do those things which exceed the power of nature. A great faith can open heaven. It can overcome the world, 1 John 5:4. It can master an easily-besetting sin, 2 Samuel 22:24. It can prefer the glory of God before secular interest, Romans 9:1. It can rejoice in af-

fliction, 1 Thessalonians 1:6. It can bridle the intemperance of passion; it can shine forth in the hemisphere of its relations; it can do duties in a more refined, sublimated manner, mixing love with duty, which mellows it and makes it taste more pleasant. It can antedate glory and make things at the greatest distance to unite. Thus the springhead of faith rises higher than nature. A man, by the power of nature, can no more do this than iron can of itself swim or the earth ascend.

3. A great faith is firm and steadfast; weak faith is frequently shaken with fears and doubt. A great faith is like an oak that spreads its roots deep and is not easily blown down, Colossians 2:7. A great faith is like the anchor or cable of a ship that holds it steady in the midst of storms. A Christian who is steeled with this heroic faith is settled in the mysteries of religion. The Spirit of God has so firmly printed heavenly truths upon his heart that you may as well remove the sun out of the firmament as remove him from those holy principles he has imbibed. Behold here a pillar in the temple of God, Revelation 3:12.

4. A great faith can trust in an angry God; it believes God's love through a frown. A vigorous faith, though it is repulsed and beaten back, yet will come on again and press upon God with a holy obstinancy. The woman of Canaan was three times repuled by Christ, yet she would take no denial from Him. She turned discouragements into arguments and made a fresh onset upon Christ until at last, by the power of faith, she overcame Him. "O woman, great is thy faith; be it unto thee even as thou wilt," Matthew 15:28. The key of her faith unlocked

Christ's heart, and now she may have what she will
from Him. When once she had gotten His heart, she
might have His treasure too.

5. A great faith can swim against the tide. It can
go cross to sense and reason. Corrupt faith says, as
Peter, "Master, pity Thyself." Faith says, "It is better
to suffer than to sin." Reason consults safety; faith
will hazard safety to preserve sanctity. A believer can
sail to heaven, though the tide of reason and the
wind of tempation are against him.

Abraham, in the case of sacrificing his son, did
not call reason to the council board. When God
said, "Offer up your son, Isaac," it was enough to
pose not only fleshly wisdom, but even faith too. For
here, the commands of God seemed to interfere. In
one command, the Lord said, "Thou shalt not murder," and, behold, here a quite contrary command,
"Offer up thy son." So that Abraham in obeying one
command seemed to disobey another. Besides, Isaac
was a son of the promise. The Messiah was to come
of Isaac's line, Hebrews 11:18. And if he was cast off,
how would the world have a Mediator? Here was
enough to puzzle this holy patriarch. Yet, Abraham's
faith unties all these knots and the bloody knife is
made ready.

Abraham believed that when God called for it, it
was not murder but sacrifice, and that the Lord, having made a promise of Christ's springing up out of
Isaac's loins, rather than the promise should fall to
the ground, God could raise up seed out of Isaac's
ashes. Here was a giant faith, which God Himself set
a trophy of honor upon. "By Myself I have sworn,
saith the Lord, for because thou hast done this

thing, and hast not withheld thy son, thine only son, that in blessing I will bless thee," Genesis 22:16.

6. A great faith can bear great delays. Though God does not give a immediate answer to prayer, faith believes it shall have an answer in due time. A weak faith is soon out of breath and, if it does not have the mercy immediately, it begins to faint. Whereas he who has a strong, powerful faith does not make haste, Isaiah 28:16. A great faith is content to stay God's leisure. Faith will trade with God for time.

"Lord," says faith, "if I do not have the mercy I want instantly, I will trust longer. I know my money is in good hands. An answer of peace will come. Perhaps the mercy is not yet ripe or, perhaps, I am not ripe for the mercy. Lord, do as it seems good in Thine eyes."

Faith knows the most tedious voyages have the richest returns, and, the longer mercy is in expectation, the sweeter it will be in fruition. Behold here a glorious faith. If we have such a faith as this to show, it is a blessed fruit of our sacramental converse with God.

But I would not discourage infant believers. If your grace is not risen to the bigness and proportion of a great faith, but is of the proper kind, it shall find acceptance. God, who bids us receive Him who is weak in faith, Romans 14:1, will not Himself refuse him. If your faith is not grown to a cedar, yet is a bruised reed, it is too good to be broken, Matthew 12:20. A weak faith can lay hold on a strong Christ. A palsied hand may tie the knot in marriage.

Only do not let Christians rest in lower measures

of grace, but aspire after higher degrees. The
stronger our faith, the firmer our union with Christ
and the more sweet influence we draw from Him.
This is that which honors the blessed Sacrament,
when we can show the increase of grace and, being
strong in faith, bring glory to God, Romans 4:20.

BRANCH 7. Has Christ provided such a blessed
banquet for us? He does not nurse us abroad, but
feeds us with His own breast, nay, His own blood.
Let us, then, study to answer this great love of Christ.
It is true, we can never parallel His love. Yet let us
show ourselves thankful. We can do nothing satis-
factory, but we may do something gratulatory. Christ
gave Himself as a sin offering for us. Let us give ourselves as a thank offering for Him. If a man redeems
another out of debt, will he not be grateful? How
deeply do we stand obliged to Christ, who has re-
deemed us from hell!

Let us show thankfulness four ways:

1. By courage. Christ has set us a copy. He did not
fear men, but endured the cross and despised the
shame. Let us be steeled with courage, being made
ready to suffer for Christ, which is, as Chrysostom
said, to be baptized with a baptism of blood. Did
Christ bear the wrath of God for us, and shall we not
bear the wrath of men for Him? It is our glory to suffer in Christ's quarrel. "The Spirit of God and of
glory resteth upon you," 1 Peter 4:14. Let us pray for
furnace grace. Be like those three children. "Be it
known to thee, O king, that we will not serve thy
gods," Daniel 3:18. They would rather burn than
bow. Oh, that such a spirit as was in Cyprian might

survive in us! The proconsul would have tempted him for his religion and said to him, "Consult for your safety." Cyprian responded, "In so just a cause, there needs no consultation." When the sentence of his death was read, he replied, "Thanks be to God."

We do not know how soon an hour of temptation may come. Oh, remember, Christ's body was broken! His blood poured out. We have no such blood to shed for Him as He shed for us.

2. Let us show our thankfulness to Christ by fruitfulness. Let us bring forth the sweet fruits of patience, heavenly-mindedness, and good works. This is to live unto Him who died for us, 2 Corinthians 5:15. If we would rejoice the heart of Christ, and make Him not to repent of His sufferings, let us be fertile in obedience. The wise men not only worshiped Christ, but presented unto Him gifts, gold and frankincense, Matthew 2:11. Let us present Christ with the best fruits of our garden. Let us give Him our love, that flower of delight. The saints are not only compared to stars for their knowledge, but spice trees for their fertileness. The breasts of the spouse were like clusters of grapes, Song of Solomon 7:7. The blood of Christ received in a spiritual manner is like the water of jealousy, which had a virtue both to kill and to make fruitful, Numbers 5:27-28. Christ's blood kills sin and makes the hearts fructify in grace.

3. Let us show our thankfulness to Christ by our zeal. How zealous was Christ for our redemption! Zeal turns a saint into a seraphim. A true Christian has a double baptism, one of water, the other of fire. He is baptized with the fire of zeal. Be zealous for

Christ's name and worship. Zeal is increased by op-
position. It cuts its way through the rocks. Zeal loves
truth most when it is disgraced and hated. "They
have made void Thy law; therefore I love Thy commandments above gold," Psalm 119:126-127.

How little thankfulness do they show to Christ
who have no zeal for His honor and interest! They
are like Ephraim. "Ephraim is a cake not turned,"
Hosea 7:8, baked on one side and dough on the
other. Christ most abominates a lukewarm temper,
Revelation 3:15. He is even sick of such professors.
Those who write of the situation of England say that
it is seated between the torrid and frigid zone. The
climate is neither very hot nor cold. I wish this were
not the temper of the people and that our hearts
were not too like the climate we live in. May the
Lord cause the fire of holy zeal to always be burning
upon the altar of our hearts.

4. Let us show our thankfulness by universal sub-
jection to Christ. This is to make the Lord's Supper,
in a spiritual sense, a feast of dedication, when we
renew our vows and give ourselves up to God's service. "Truly I am Thy servant, I am Thy servant,"
Psalm 116:16. "Lord, all I have is Thine. My head
shall be Thine to study for Thee; my hands shall be
Thine to work for Thee; my heart shall be Thine to
adore Thee; my tongue shall be Thine to praise
Thee."

BRANCH 8. If Jesus Christ has provided so holy
an ordinance as the Sacrament, let us walk suitably
to it. Have we received Christ into our hearts? Let us
show Him forth by our heavenliness.

Let us show forth Christ by our heavenly words. Let us speak the language of Canaan. When the Holy Ghost came upon the apostles, they spoke with other tongues, Acts 2:4. While we speak the words of grace and soberness, our lips smell like perfume and drip like honey.

Let us show forth Christ by our heavenly affections. Let our sighs and breathings after God go up as a cloud of incense. "Set your affections on things above," Colossians 3:2. We should do by our affectiosn as the husbandmen do by their corn. If the corn lies low in a damp room, it is in danger of corruption. Therefore, they carry it up into their highest room that it may keep the better. So our affections, if set on earth, are apt to corrupt and be unsavory. Therefore, we should carry them up on high above the world that they may be preserved pure. Breathe after fuller revelations of God. Desire to attain unto the resurrection of the dead, Philippians 3:11. The higher our affections are raised towards heaven, the sweeter joys we feel. The higher the lark flies, the sweeter it sings.

Let us show forth Christ by our heavenly conversation, Philippians 3:20. Hypocrites may, in a pang of conscience, have some good affections stirred, but they are as flushes of heat in the face which come and go. But the constant tenor of our life must be holy. We must shine forth in a kind of angelic sanctity. As it is with a piece of coin, it does not have only the king's image within a ring but his superscription without. So it is not enough to have the image of Christ in the heart, but there must be the superscription without. Something of Christ must be written in the life.

The scandalous lives of many communicants are a reproach to the Sacrament and tempt others to infidelity. How odious it is that those hands which have received the sacramental elements should take bribes! That those eyes which have been filled with tears at the Lord's Table should, afterwards, be filled with envy! That those teeth, which have eaten holy bread, should grind the faces of the poor! That those lips, which have touched the sacramental cup, should salute a harlot! That the mouth which has drunk consecrated wine should be full of oaths! That they who seem to deify Christ in the eucharist should vilify Him in His members! In a word, that such as pretend to eat Christ's body and drink His blood at church should eat the bread of wickedness and drink the wine of violence in their own houses, Proverbs 4:17. These are like those Italians I have read of who, at the Sacrament, are so devout, as if they believed God to be in the bread, but in their lives are so profane, as if they did not believe God to be in heaven. Such as these are apt to make the world think that the gospel is but a fancy or a religious cheat. What shall I say of them? With Judas, they receive the devil in the sop, and are no better than crucifiers of the Lord of glory. As their sin is heinous, so their punishment will be proportionable. "They eat and drink damnation to themselves," 1 Corinthians 11:29.

Oh, that such a luster and majesty of holiness sparkled forth in the lives of communicants, so that others would say, "These have been with Jesus!" And their consciences may lie under the power of this conviction, that the Sacrament has a confirming and a transforming virtue in it!

USE 4. Comfort to God's people.

1. From Christ's broken body and His blood poured out, we may gather this comfort, that it was a glorious sacrifice.

It was a sacrifice of infinite merit. Had it been only an angel that suffered, or had Christ been only a mere man, as some blasphemously dream, then we might have despaired of salvation. But He suffered for us who was God as well as man. Therefore, the apostle expressly calls it "the blood of God," Acts 20:28. It is man that sins. It is God in our nature that dies. This is sovereign medicine to believers. Christ having poured out His blood, now God's justice is completely satisfied. God was infinitely more content with Christ's sufferings upon mount Calvary than if we had lain in hell and undergone His wrath forever. The blood of Christ has quenched the flame of Divine fury. And, now, what should we fear? All are enemies are either reconciled or subdued. God is a reconciled enemy, and sin is a subdued enemy. "Who shall lay anything to the charge of God's elect? It is Christ that died," Romans 8:34. When the devil accuses us, let us show him the cross of Christ. When he brings his pencil and goes to paint our sin in their colors, let us bring the sponge of Christ's blood, and that will wipe them out again. All bonds are cancelled. Whatever the law has charged upon us is discharged. The debt book is crossed with the blood of the Lamb.

It was a sacrifice of eternal extent. The benefit of

it is perpetuated. "He entered in once into the holy
place, having obtained eternal redemption for us,"
Hebrews 9:12. Therefore, Christ is said to be a Priest
forever, Hebrews 5:6, because the virtue and comfort
of His sacrifice abides forever.

2. Christ's blood being shed, believers may lay
claim to all heavenly privileges. Wills are ratified by
the death of the testator. "A testament is of force after men are dead," Hebrews 9:17. It is observable in
the text that Christ calls His blood "the blood of the
New Testament." Christ made a will or testament,
and gave rich legacies to the saints: pardon of sin,
grace, and glory. The Scriptures are the rolls
wherein these legacies are registered. Christ's blood
is the sealing of the will. This blood being shed,
Christians may put in for a title to these legacies.

"Lord, pardon my sin. Christ has died for my
pardon. Give me grace; Christ has purchased it by
His blood."

The testator being dead, the will is in force.
Christian, are you not filled with joy? Are you not
possessed of heaven? Yet you have this confirmed by
will. A man who has a deed sealed, making over
such lands and tenements after the expiration of a
few years, though at present he has little to help
himself with, yet he comforts himself when he looks
upon his sealed deed with hopes of that which is to
come. So though at present we do not enjoy the privileges of consolation and glorification, yet we may
cheer our hearts with this: The deed is sealed; the
will and testament is ratified by the blood shedding
of Christ.

3. Is Christ's blood shed? Here is comfort against

death. A dying Savior sweetens the pangs of death. Is your Lord crucified? Be of good comfort. Christ, by dying, has overcome death. He has cut the lock of sin where the strength of death lay. Christ has knocked out the teeth of this lion. He has pulled the thorn out of death so that it cannot prick a believer's conscience. "O death, I will be thy plague," Hosea 13:14. Christ has disarmed death and taken away all its deadly weapons so that, though it may strike, it cannot sting a believer. Christ has drawn the poison out of death. Nay, He has made death friendly. This pale horse carries a child of God home to his Father's house. Faith gives a right to heaven; death gives us possession. What sweet comfort may we draw from the crucifixion of our Lord! His precious blood makes the pale face of death to be of a ruddy and beautiful complexion.

USE 5. Here is a dark side of the cloud to all profane persons who live and die in sin. They have no part in Christ's blood. Their condition will be worse than if Christ had not died. Christ, who is a loadstone to draw the elect to heaven, will be a millstone to sink the wicked deeper in hell. There is a crew of sinners who slight Christ's blood and swear by it. Let them know His blood will cry against them. They must feel the same wrath which Christ felt upon the cross. And, because they cannot bear it at once, they must be undergoing it to eternity, 2 Thessalonians 1:9. So inconceivably torturing will this be that the damned do not know how to endure it, nor yet how to avoid it.

Sinners will not believe this until it is too late.

Wicked men, while they live, are blinded by the god of this world. But, when they are dying, the eye of their consciences will begin to be opened and they shall see the wrath of God flaming before their eyes, which sight will be but a sad prologue to an eternal tragedy.

Other Works by Thomas Watson published by Soli Deo Gloria

Heaven Taken by Storm. This is one of our most popular books. Here Watson shows that men are to take heaven by "holy violence." He shows how we are to storm the gates of heaven by prayer, by reading God's Word, by attending on His ordinances, and by self-examination and self-denial. This work is short, readable, and challenging. ($12.95)

A Plea for the Godly. This is a collection of 19 sermons by Thomas Watson, most of which have never been reprinted until now. Some of these are: Watson's analysis of Romanism, his farewell prayer and sermon to his congregation at St. Stephen's Walbrook just before his ejection for non-conformity, his sermon on "Comfort for the Church of God," his sermon on the right use of the tongue, and the title sermon, that a righteous man is more excellent than his neighbor. The cover is a beautifully painted portrait of Watson preaching from his pulpit. Nearly 500 pages. ($32.95)

The Sermons of Thomas Watson. In 1826, most of Watson's longer treatises were compiled in a two volume set. This work was called *The Select Works of Thomas Watson.* It included his classic work on the Beatitudes, as well as "The Christian's Charter," "The Saints' Spiritual Delight," "Christ's Loveliness," "The Upright Man's Character," and many others. We have combined the two volumes into one and eliminated the sermons on the Beatitudes, which has already been published by the Banner of Truth. This volume is over 700 pages in length. ($29.95)

The Duty of Self-Denial. This is a collection of scarce writings from the pen of this much beloved Puritan pastor. There are 10 other sermons such as "The Peace of Christ", "The Good Shepherd", "The Day of Judgment Asserted", and "The Comforting Rod." This hardback volume is over 200 pages long. ($22.95)

The Art of Divine Contentment. This is one of Watson's finest and most popular works. It is a treatment of Philippians 4:11, over 250 pages. ($24.95)

Gleanings from Thomas Watson. Here are 150 pages of short, pithy extracts from the writings and sermons of Thomas Watson. This is a fine introductory volume to give those who are not familiar with the Puritans, but are not ready to tackle an entire volume. These extracts are categorized by subject headings to make them easy to find and easy to use. Great for pastors to use in sermon preparation! ($16.95)